Writing Effectively in Print and on the Web

PRACTICAL GUIDES FOR LIBRARIANS

⊚ About the Series

This innovative series written and edited for librarians by librarians provides authoritative, practical information and guidance on a wide spectrum of library processes and operations.

Books in the series are focused, describing practical and innovative solutions to a problem facing today's librarian and delivering step-by-step guidance for planning, creating, implementing, managing, and evaluating a wide range of services and programs.

The books are aimed at beginning and intermediate librarians needing basic instruction/ guidance in a specific subject and at experienced librarians who need to gain knowledge in a new area or guidance in implementing a new program/service.

⊚ About the Series Editor

The **Practical Guides for Librarians** series was conceived by and is edited by M. Sandra Wood, MLS, MBA, AHIP, FMLA, Librarian Emerita, Penn State University Libraries.

M. Sandra Wood was a librarian at the George T. Harrell Library, The Milton S. Hershey Medical Center, College of Medicine, Pennsylvania State University, Hershey, PA, for over 35 years, specializing in reference, educational, and database services. Ms. Wood worked for several years as a Development Editor for Neal-Schuman Publishers.

Ms. Wood received an MLS from Indiana University and an MBA from the University of Maryland. She is a Fellow of the Medical Library Association and served as a member of MLA's Board of Directors from 1991 to 1995. Ms. Wood is founding and current editor of *Medical Reference Services Quarterly*, now in its 35th volume. She also was founding editor of the *Journal of Consumer Health on the Internet* and the *Journal of Electronic Resources in Medical Libraries* and served as editor/co-editor of both journals through 2011.

Titles in the Series

1. *How to Teach: A Practical Guide for Librarians* by Beverley E. Crane
2. *Implementing an Inclusive Staffing Model for Today's Reference Services* by Julia K. Nims, Paula Storm, and Robert Stevens
3. *Managing Digital Audiovisual Resources: A Practical Guide for Librarians* by Matthew C. Mariner
4. *Outsourcing Technology: A Practical Guide for Librarians* by Robin Hastings
5. *Making the Library Accessible for All: A Practical Guide for Librarians* by Jane Vincent

Writing Effectively in Print and on the Web

A Practical Guide for Librarians

Rebecca Blakiston

PRACTICAL GUIDES FOR LIBRARIANS, NO. 30

ROWMAN & LITTLEFIELD
Lanham • Boulder • New York • London

Published by Rowman & Littlefield
A wholly owned subsidiary of The Rowman & Littlefield Publishing Group, Inc.
4501 Forbes Boulevard, Suite 200, Lanham, Maryland 20706
www.rowman.com

Unit A, Whitacre Mews, 26-34 Stannary Street, London SE11 4AB

British Library Cataloguing in Publication Information Available

Library of Congress Cataloging-in-Publication Data Available

978-1-4422-7885-1 (pbk : alk. paper)
978-1-4422-7886-8 (electronic)

♾™ The paper used in this publication meets the minimum requirements of American
National Standard for Information Sciences—Permanence of Paper for Printed Library
Materials, ANSI/NISO Z39.48-1992.

Printed in the United States of America

To Gibberz Doodle Bean, aka "The Gibbs,"

who brought so much joy to our lives.

She's barking at angels now.

Contents

List of Tables

Preface

Writing plays a role in almost everything we do. It's how we document our knowledge, share our stories, and ask our communities for help. It's a tool to teach, influence, and persuade those around us. And in today's digital age, we're all publishers, sharing content with the world at the push of a button (literally). From webpages, to signage, to emails—writing is fundamental to our everyday lives.

Sadly, there's a lot of mediocre content out there: policy-driven websites with mountains of text, building signs that don't actually tell you what you need to know, convoluted emails that leave you wondering , *What was the point of that?* Today's reader is bombarded with endless streams of information and simply doesn't have time to sift through and make sense of it all.

Let's do our part to end the madness. *Writing Effectively in Print and on the Web: A Practical Guide for Librarians* encourages you to put your readers at the heart of all your content, ensuring that it is engaging, relevant, and useful. You'll learn techniques to write with clarity, precision, and purpose, which will serve you well in both your professional and your personal life.

I truly enjoyed writing this book. I've always enjoyed nonfiction writing—studying English in college and taking pride in my analytical essays and argumentative papers. When my career path led me to focus on user experience, I quickly learned the power of the written word in the context of service and product design. At the University of Arizona Libraries, I've led our website content efforts for the past five years—creating an editorial style guide, voice and tone standards, and comprehensive training for all web content writers in the library. When I organized the User Experience Certificate for Library Juice Academy, I included courses on both writing for the web and content strategy. As my role evolved at the University of Arizona, I recognized the massive content challenges ahead and hired a full-time content strategist. Now with us for three years, our content strategist focuses on creating and sustaining quality written content on the website and beyond.

There are, of course, many books on the craft of writing. There are the classics like *Elements of Style* by William Strunk and E. B. White and *Writing Well* by William Zinsser. You can also find shelves of books on business writing, plain-language writing, technical writing, and professional writing. And today you can find books that speak directly to writing for the digital age, two of my favorites being *Letting Go of the Words:*

Writing Web Content That Works, by Janice (Ginny) Redish, and *Everybody Writes: Your Go-To Guide to Creating Ridiculously Good Content*, by Ann Handley.

But there still aren't many books focused on user-centered writing within the context of educational institutions such as libraries. *Writing Effectively in Print and on the Web: A Practical Guide for Librarians* places us in the world of the library, an often content-rich, process-driven, jargon-filled world. As librarians, we carry with us unique struggles. We lack time and resources. We tend to have numerous content authors across the organization. We must balance our altruistic mission of sharing knowledge with our duty to make readers' lives easier, creating content that is substantive, yet concise.

This book is geared toward librarians but is useful for anyone who desires to become a better writer. It's written for people with no editorial background, but it also contains information for the more adept writers looking for advice and inspiration on how to approach their work.

I have organized the book into chapters that allow for easy skimming. While I encourage you to read the book in its entirety, it's not necessary to do so, or to read the chapters in order. If you're starting a new writing project, however, I do recommend you read chapters 2 and 3 before diving into the rest.

In chapter 1, you'll discover the power of good writing. In chapters 2 and 3, you'll identify the audience and the purpose of your content, foundational steps for any writing project. In chapters 4 and 5, you'll master the basic principles of good writing: keeping it simple, purposeful, active, and authentic. Next, in chapters 6 and 7, you will experiment with different elements to better structure your content, including titles, headings, lists, and tables. Then in chapters 8–11, you'll learn techniques for unique writing challenges such as instructions, forms, webpages, and emails.

We'll have a bit of fun in chapter 12, where you'll consider ways to incorporate personality and emotion into your writing through voice and tone. With writing techniques in hand, in chapter 13 you'll find out how better formatting decisions will allow your content to shine. In chapter 14 we'll put it all together, exploring the process of writing and ways to continue honing your craft.

There is no one way to write, but there is a better way to write. This book is as advertised: a practical guide filled with real-life examples along with methods you can put into practice immediately. My hope is that it will arm you with the tools to convey information with the greatest possible clarity. I'd love for you to put this on your bookshelf and refer to it often.

I want all of us to sharpen, tighten, and energize our writing—and have fun doing it. I wrote this book over the course of a year, so I apologize for its length. I empathize with Ben Franklin, who once wrote, "I have already made this paper too long, for which I must crave pardon, not having now time to make it shorter" (1760: 82).

Reference

Franklin, Benjamin. 1760. *New Experiments and Observations on Electricity. Made at Philadelphia in America. By Benjamin Franklin, Esq; and communicated in several letters to Peter Collinson, Esq; of London, F.R.S. Part I.* 2003 electronic reproduction. Farmington Hills, MI: Thomson Gale.

Acknowledgments

Taking on a second book was kind of crazy, and taking on a book about writing was even crazier. I didn't know it when I signed up, but writing about writing is one of the hardest things to do. So I want to thank everyone who made it possible for me to get through this, emerging on the other side with my sanity intact and with a book I'm actually pretty proud of.

First, thanks to the staff of Rowman & Littlefield. Sandy Wood, we've both had a rough go lately, but you're the best editor I could imagine working with. And Charles Harmon, I appreciate your continued support and encouragement more than you know.

Thank you to authors before me who provided guidance and inspiration. Ginny Redish, your seminal book on web writing was my first introduction to the field and got me hooked. I am eternally grateful that you agreed to come to Tucson a few years back to share your passion and expertise. Ann Handley, your book on writing good content had me literally clapping and laughing out loud. I want everyone to read your book and commit it to memory. And to every other author cited—thank you for sharing your knowledge with the world.

Back in library land, thanks to Nicole Capdarest-Arest for loving the written word as much (if not more) than I do, and for cocreating and teaching the web writing course for Library Juice Academy. And a huge shout-out to like-minded colleagues near and far: Suzanne Chapman, Heidi Steiner Burkhardt, Anne Haines, Conny Liegl, Nadaleen Tempelman-Kluit, Kim Vassiliadis, Emily Daly, Jill Heinze, Rachel Vacek, Beth Filar Williams, Erin White, Stephanie Hartman, Kristian Serrano, Joe Marquez, SuHui Ho, Michael Schofield, Amanda Goodman, and Courtney Greene McDonald. I'm impressed by your continued advocacy for the user experience, and together we're slowly but surely fostering a culture of user-centered design (and content) in libraries worldwide.

Thank you to my web-design and user-experience colleagues who inspire me daily and put up with my book-writing nonsense, which seems to never end. Shoshana Mayden, you're making sustainable, consistent, user-driven content a reality across the library. And you still have time to provide me with editorial help—I can't thank you enough! Ginger Bidwell, you work tirelessly to affect the lives of students, faculty, and staff, taking on any challenge that comes your way—and I'm forever appreciative. Taylor Sturges, your commitment to continued improvement of the library is evident, and your positive spirit lifts the team in ways I bet you don't even realize. Rui Qi, you are a fantastic addition to our team, bringing creativity and dedication to your work—I'm so excited to see what great things we can do. Cameron Wiles, in short time you've dived into our websites and improved all kinds of content—your commitment to sentence-case titles and parallel construction confirms that you chose the right job! Donovan Pete, I'm so glad you've recently joined our team and look forward to seeing how you improve design in libraries now and in the future.

Huge appreciation also goes to the dev team—Mike Hagedon, Will Simpson, and Jeffrey Turman—my partners in design + dev crime. You question assumptions, continually improve your process, and connect every line of code to how it might affect humans on the other end. You truly care about the user experience, and that's pretty awesome. I couldn't ask for a better team to collaborate with every day.

Thanks to my former colleagues who have moved on to greener pastures but whose contributions live on. Beau Smith, you were an exceptional employee, relentlessly dedicated to improving the user experience through research and testing. You're going to go far and I can't wait to collaborate in the future. Andrew See, you were integral to the website steering group, and I'm so glad we converted you to the one-space-after-periods rule. I'm sure you're doing great things with our neighbors to the far north. Bonnie Jean Michalski, you cared about content as much as any of us and shared in my love of a good idiom. I wish you happiness and success and look forward to catching up when you next visit Tucson.

And thank you to others in the library who made this book possible. Jeremy Frumkin, I appreciate your support as I hammered through fourteen chapters and your flexibility as I organized my often-scattered work schedule. Thanks to everyone who provided examples that are sprinkled throughout the book, including Shelly Black, Michael Brewer, and Kylie Rogers. And eternal gratitude goes to my colleagues who listened to my tirades, empathized with my struggles, and encouraged me to persist and move forward: Yvonne Mery, Niamh Wallace, Teresa Hazen, Elizabeth Kline, Annabelle Nuñez, Cheryl Cuillier, Travis Teetor, and Shannon Jones.

On a personal note, I express deep appreciation to my family for their continued encouragement: Mom, Dad, Jessica, Nick, and Gwen. And even Annabelle, Henry, and Chips—you might not be able to articulate your support, but your presence brings great joy to my life and makes everything just a little bit better.

Last but not least, thanks to Scott Ware, my supportive and loving husband. Scott, in the relatively short course of writing this book, we went through significant life events: our wedding and honeymoon, Gibby's lymphoma and euthanasia, your hospitalization and two surgeries, and an exploding ceiling fan. Throughout it all, your love, patience, and good humor kept us both going. You bring such peace and happiness to my life, and I couldn't imagine doing what I do without you by my side. You're the best.

Why Good Writing Matters

LIBRARIANS CONSTANTLY USE THE WRITTEN word to share ideas, yet too little attention is paid to the craft of good writing. Does your audience understand what you are trying to communicate, or do your words fall short? In this chapter, you'll learn why good writing matters to the success of your library as well as your own professional growth and reputation.

Writing for Users

Everyone Is a Publisher

As more content is curated and consumed digitally, it is incredibly easy to publish content to the world. Anyone who can get online can become a publisher, sharing information on webpages, by email, and through social media. It is rare to find a librarian who doesn't regularly communicate with users in some digital form.

Creating content for print has also become commonplace, no matter your professional position. Graphic programs and templates allow people with no design background to create professional-looking signs, brochures, posters, and flyers. This responsibility is often spread across units within larger libraries, rarely restricted to a marketing department or requiring a review process.

Indeed, everyone is now a publisher. Today's environment provides endless opportunities for librarians to share their messages and influence the user experience.

Write for the In-Person Experience

You can find written communication throughout library buildings, primarily through print and digital signage. Look around your library. You likely have instructional content on your walls, such as how to:

- Return a book
- Pick up a hold
- Use a self-checkout machine
- Access compact shelving
- Sign up for a computer
- Book a study room
- Print from a computer station
- Use a scanner

Most libraries also have signage about building rules. These signs explain your policies and code of conduct, letting visitors know what they can and cannot do. This might include content about:

- Quiet sections or floors
- Cell phone use
- Food and drink
- Smoking, pets, and weapons

Service desks are likely signposted. In addition to the name of the desk, you might have content related to services provided. For example:

- Borrow laptops here
- Book study rooms here
- Ring bell for service
- Computer rules and regulations
- No meeting rooms currently available

Directional signage is commonplace, especially in larger libraries. It can tell visitors where to find things and how to navigate within particular floors or sections. Such signage may include:

- Sections (e.g., reading room, staff offices)
- Collections (e.g., children's literature, newspapers)
- Call number signs at the end of shelving
- Signs pointing to restrooms, emergency exits, and stairs
- Floor maps and directories

Your library probably raises awareness of its offerings through promotional material on posters, digital signs, flyers, and brochures. This content may highlight:

- New services
- Services for particular audiences
- Services offered in a certain area (e.g., circulation, homework help)
- Upcoming events
- Current exhibits
- Donations and fundraising

Creative, curated content is also a mainstay in libraries and museums. If you have exhibits and other displays, you likely also have associated content such as:

- Exhibit overviews (on posters, flyers, etc.)
- Placards describing exhibit content
- Brochures about exhibits

In a single visit, a library user might encounter dozens of messages about where to go, what to do, what not to do, and how to do something. This content can make or break the visitor's experience and feelings toward the library.

In addition to content for building visitors, there is print content out there in the world. Librarians are rarely confined to their offices, often leaving the library building to interact directly with users where they work, study, and research. If you are teaching an instruction session, you might provide handouts, written assignments, or other supplemental content. If you are delivering an orientation or tour, you might have brochures, floor directories, bookmarks, or tip sheets.

Consider your own library. What content do users experience as they visit your buildings? If a librarian is visiting them at their place of work or study, what content do they get to take home with them? Is it content you're proud of? Does it represent your library in the best possible light?

Write for the Digital Experience

Libraries increasingly communicate with users through the web, so the quality of content in your digital space is critical. Your website content may include:

- Informational webpages (e.g., policies, procedures, hours, frequently asked questions)
- Task-based webpages (e.g., reserve a meeting room, chat with a librarian, make a donation)
- Forms (e.g., request an article, contact us)

You might have web presence beyond your basic website. Libraries often use third-party tools to create and/or host their content, such as:

- LibGuides for research guides
- ContentDM for digital collections
- Omeka for online exhibits
- Adobe Captivate and Articulate Storyline for tutorials
- YouTube and Vimeo for videos
- PowerPoint and SlideShare for slide decks

You may push out content to users directly. Consider content created for:

- Online newsletters
- Email notifications
- Facebook
- Twitter
- Instagram

You also likely have direct conversations with your users through email, chat, text, and social media.

Libraries of all kinds have a digital presence overflowing with written content. The online landscape keeps evolving, providing new opportunities to curate and expose content to the world. While exciting, it can become overwhelming. Are you using the online environment wisely to share your messages and engage your users?

Writing for Colleagues

Writing is an essential part of your professional career. You obviously want to provide useful content for end users, but you also need to pay attention to content you send colleagues, supervisors, administrators, stakeholders, and your broader library network.

EVERYONE COMPLAINS ABOUT EMAILS

Do you feel like you get too many work emails? Most people do. A research study found the majority of email traffic worldwide now comes from business email, accounting for over 100 billion daily (Radicati, 2013). Librarians spend countless work hours sending, receiving, and responding to emails. It has become the primary way we communicate with our colleagues, supervisors, and employees. Emails have transformed working life. Write better, more thoughtful emails and encourage others to do the same, and you will increase efficiency, reduce email overload, and improve your overall working life.

Manage Work

Written communication is key to sharing and receiving information in order to get your work done. Email and shared documents are the primary mechanisms for two-way and group communication. In addition, web-based productivity, project management, and ticketing tools can help facilitate structured communication among co-workers. Popular options include Trello, Slack, Asana, and Redmine. Such tools might be part of your daily routine and help you manage communications among team members or across different parts of the organization. Content to help manage your work may include:

- Project outlines and timelines
- Checklists

- Project definitions, including goals and scope
- Detailed responsibilities and expectations
- Meeting agendas and minutes
- Task and progress tracking
- Solicited feedback and responses
- Decisions and changes made

Effective written communication can make projects run smoother and more efficiently, create an environment for sound decision making, and ensure that feedback is given and received freely and without conflict. Structured, practical, consistent written communication makes for a happier, more productive, and more energizing place to work.

Communicate Work

Another large part of work life is providing updates on your work to colleagues and administrators. If you are a project manager, you might deliver monthly email updates on your progress. If you are a department head, you might compile annual reports that summarize your recent successes. As an individual librarian, you may write content for your performance review where you're asked to explain your work and its impact to your community.

You might use slide decks, intranet pages, or print or digital documents to deliver your message. The quality of the content will affect your colleagues' impressions of your work. This can subsequently affect your overall reputation as a professional, helping or harming your future opportunities within the organization.

Document Policies and Procedures

If you are in a role that involves training or providing support for staff, you have written materials that employees are expected to use. This includes content created for training new staff as well as functional content used to get things done. For example:

- Policies (e.g., working from home, lunch breaks)
- Procedures and how-to instructions (e.g., time reporting, email setup)
- Request forms (e.g., travel, leave, funding, IT support)
- Other forms (e.g., insurance, reimbursement)

Too often, content like this is not just dry and boring; it is cumbersome and difficult for staff to understand. If staff don't understand rules or processes they are expected to follow, it not only adds additional staff time to respond to questions but can also put their jobs on the line. To ensure understandability, review every documented policy, procedure, and form staff are required to use as part of their jobs. Each document should be clear, succinct, and leave no room for ambiguity.

Serve the Profession

If you are active in professional organizations, such as the American Library Association, you use written communication for everything from documenting meeting minutes to recruiting members to write blog posts and newsletters. This type of information can overwhelm a librarian's email inbox as content comes through multiple listservs and channels. Making thoughtful content decisions on behalf of the association will help you stand out from the clutter and get your message across. People will be more likely to read your message, making it more likely to get the response you want. This can also help you build your professional reputation.

Writing Good Content Matters

It Matters to Users

Librarians love content. After all, one of their primary missions is to provide content that is meaningful, useful, and relevant. And yet, the written content that overburdened, time-constrained librarians curate is too often put together without considering the reader and without taking the time to do it right.

Curators can put up an amazing exhibit of content, but if the explanatory content written on note cards is difficult to interpret, the exhibit loses meaning. Digital collections can be outstanding, but if the descriptions that welcome users to the collection don't speak in their language, they might leave immediately. You can have a near-perfect navigation system on your website, but then fail when it comes to the actual content—can users find the answers to their questions? Can they decipher the words on the page? Can they skim the headings and get the gist of what the webpage is all about?

The written content you provide plays an essential role in defining your library as an organization. Content can affect each part of the user journey, from the first impression a visitor has when she enters your building and reads a digital sign, to the interaction she later has on your website, to the email she reads a week later. Users have high expectations when it comes to their experience. They don't have much time to decipher content and they want to quickly complete tasks and find answers to their questions. They also want to feel a sense of belonging, be treated respectfully, and be inspired to discover new knowledge. Written content provides an enormous opportunity to connect with your users, make them feel welcome, and leave a positive lasting impression.

It Matters to Colleagues

Too often, even less thought is put into written communication with colleagues. Cryptic email responses are sent haphazardly, reports are put together without thoughtful headings and structure, and meeting minutes go on for five pages without any articulated next steps or outcomes. The writer is then surprised to learn that her supervisor misunderstood the purpose of her email, her colleague wasn't aware of the current status of a project, or her employee didn't realize he was supposed to send her feedback.

How many times have you seen an email and immediately disregarded it as unimportant or irrelevant? Do you think the writer would have thought it was relevant to you? Have you ever found out after disregarding something that you were in fact supposed to do something? Librarians receive a vast amount of content daily, and it can be hard to pull out what is relevant and worthwhile. Too often, requests for feedback or other calls to action are hidden within a large body of content that readers are skimming over. Composing your content thoughtfully will ensure that important messages don't get lost. You'll also be building better relationships with your colleagues by respecting their time.

Everybody has different styles and strengths when it comes to writing. Upon quick reflection, you might be able to identify the people you work with that have the most problematic written communication. Why?

- Are their sentences or paragraphs too long?
- Do they send out content that seems irrelevant to the audience?
- Do they overcomplicate things, making them difficult to decipher or take action upon?
- Is their content vague or without clear purpose?
- Do they use passive voice?
- Do they use jargon or formal language that makes the message hard to decipher?

On the other end of the spectrum, you probably have colleagues who are excellent communicators. What is it that makes them stand out? Pay attention to their approaches:

- Are they using subject lines more effectively?
- Are they structuring their documents with headings?
- Do they use tables and bullets to make content more easily digestible?
- Do they make it clear when they want feedback or some other action?
- Are their sentences concise and direct?
- Do they get to the point more quickly than others?

Start studying the communications you receive from colleagues. Take notice of what works well for you as a reader and what fails. One of the best ways to become a better writer is to study what you read.

◎ Writing for Digital and Print

Reading in the Digital Age

The prevalence of reading on a computer screen has affected reading behavior over the past couple of decades. It's long been realized that readers tend to scan online content, reading perhaps 20 percent of a webpage (Nielsen, 2008). But this habit is no longer limited to online content. In fact, reading on-screen is fostering a "snippet" approach to the written word in general, where readers primarily skim content and spend much less time in deep concentration (Baron, 2015).

As librarians are fully aware, there is an ongoing debate of the benefits and preferences for e-books versus print books. People argue that readers will tend to skim an e-book whereas they will slowly read and more fully process information in a print book. This is partially true, but the environment is a moving target. The line between print and digital is now fuzzy. A Kindle, for example, mimics the look of print—it doesn't have the glare that a traditional computer screen will have, nor does it have the distractions of other devices (e.g., notifications, Internet). Digital signs are physical objects with no user interaction. Most print pieces were born digital. Many publications are both printed and placed online.

While there are continued studies on slow or deep reading, focused attention, and the brain, it cannot be denied that as a writer, you should expect to have your readers' attention only for a short period of time. In the digital and information age, readers are rarely concentrating on your content for more than a few moments. To make an impact and get your messages across, it's more important than ever to write with the reader in mind.

Differences in Digital and Print Structure

Digital and print content differs in its functionality. In the digital environment, you can create a sophisticated structure. The web allows you to use tools with semantic meaning, including hierarchical headings, tiers of navigation, and HTML tags (such as <strong>). The web is interactive and can include links between content, expandable content, and functionality such as hover and drag-and-drop. These possibilities will influence how you approach the organization of your web content. Something produced solely in print has none of these capabilities. The only interaction a user might have with print is turning a page (book), flipping it over (flyer), or opening it up (brochure).

That said, writing well is writing well. It is equally important in print as it is on the web. Writing in plain language and ensuring your written content is organized and understandable, as well as being engaging and compelling, are important whatever the format.

◉ Learning to Write Well

Writing Is a Craft, Not an Art

Some people are better writers than others, but people aren't born good writers. It takes effort. Better writing comes with intentional practice, critique, reflection, and revision. As Zinsser explains, "Writing is a craft, not an art. . . . If your job is to write every day, you learn to do it like any other job" (2006: 4).

Better writing also comes by paying attention to your surroundings. As you go about your day, notice where language is used in your environment. Read junk mail, terms of use agreements, billboards, signs, and brochures. What works and what doesn't, and *why*? What makes you confused? What makes you lose trust in an organization? What makes you happy? What makes you feel informed and empowered? Spend time critiquing content in your daily life, and you'll pick up new ideas, tricks, and inspiration for your own work.

There Is No Right Way

Writing is not an exact science. There is no right way to write, and there are few hard-and-fast rules when it comes to writing, especially in an informal context. While this book points out some better ways to write, it doesn't claim to know all the answers and certainly doesn't claim you must follow certain rules *all of the time*. Rules are made to be broken, and the English language is a constantly evolving system. You will write differently from your parents, your colleagues, and your friends. And that's a good thing. Writing is a deeply personal, human behavior and reflects who you are as an individual.

Your writing process might also differ from others, and that's normal. Zinsser understood that different approaches aren't just to be expected; they are inevitable. He writes, "Some people write by day, others by night. Some people need silence, others turn on the radio. Some write by hand, some by computer, some by talking into a tape recorder.

Some people write their first draft in one long burst and then revise; others can't write the second paragraph until they have fiddled endlessly with the first" (2006: 5). Discover what process works well for you. Embrace your writing strengths and work tirelessly to improve your writing weaknesses. Dedicate time to improving your craft. Whatever you do, remain open to critique and new approaches to writing as you learn and grow as a professional.

⊚ Key Points

Good writing builds stronger, more effective relationships with your users and your colleagues. It reflects your library's identity and your personal brand, and is a core part of the user experience. Remember:

- Good writing saves your users time.
- Good writing improves your work life.
- The digital environment makes good writing as important as ever.
- There is no right way to write.

If you are committed to writing well, you have to pay attention to your audience. Next, you will find out how to get to know your readers.

⊚ References

Baron, Naomi. 2015. "The Plague of tl;dr." *The Chronicle Review*, February 9. http://chronicle.com/article/The-Plague-of-tl-dr/151635.

Nielsen, Jakob. 2008. "How Little Do Users Read?" Nielsen Norman Group. May 6. www.nngroup.com/articles/how-little-do-users-read.

Radicati, Sara, ed. 2013. "Email Statistics Report, 2013-2017." The Radicati Group, Inc. April 1. www.radicati.com/wp/wp-content/uploads/2013/04/Email-Statistics-Report-2013-2017-Executive-Summary.pdf.

Zinsser, William. 2006. *On Writing Well: The Classic Guide to Writing Nonfiction.* New York: Harper & Row.

Knowing Your Readers

THE FIRST STEP TO BETTER WRITING is empathizing with your readers. In this chapter, you will discover how to get to know your readers, why it's so important, and how to consider them in everything you write.

Knowing Your Readers Matters

Readers Are the Whole Point

Unless you are writing a personal journal, you probably intend for somebody to read your content. You translate your thoughts into words and write them down, and then it becomes another person's job to read and understand those words. The value of writing is not in the author's own personal enjoyment (although that's a plus). The value is that that somebody is able to read it, get something out of it, and do something with it. Stephen King writes, "The reader must always be your main concern; without Constant Reader, you are just a voice quacking in the void" (2000: 124).

Why spend the time writing something if no one is going to want to read it? Adopt a user-centered approach. It will help you evaluate your writing with a more critical eye, and you will ultimately write better, more compelling, and more useful content.

Readers Will Understand Your Writing

You have intention behind your writing, and you want your readers to understand your message. You have a much better chance of this happening if you have a strong sense of who your readers are and where they are coming from. Ross and Nilsen explain, "Your readers will have to interpret your text, and their interpretation will be colored by many factors, including their relationship to you, their roles, their skill at reading, their knowledge of the topic at hand, their previous experiences, expectations, and biases, and their goals in reading the text" (2013: 63–64). Paying attention to these factors will help you make better content decisions. By understanding the characteristics and perspectives of your audience, you are more likely to:

- Frame content within the appropriate context
- Choose words that make sense to your readers
- Anticipate and answer your readers' questions
- Avoid or explain any jargon

Combined, these practices will produce better, more understandable content. You are more likely to meet your own goals and the goals of your readers.

WRITING FOR HUMANS

Another advantage to keeping your readers in mind is that you are more likely to address them directly, as you would actual people. In future chapters, you'll learn the benefits of using active voice and conversational language. Empathizing with your readers and writing to them directly will guarantee more conversational, human-centered language.

You Will Better Represent Your Library (or Yourself)

Libraries have long valued customer service. Significant resources are spent on training frontline staff to be friendly, knowledgeable, and respectful. Meeting and exceeding customer expectations is a great way to build a strong community of users that trust you, support you, and see the value in the services you provide. Poorly constructed content that doesn't consider the audience works against your customer service mission. It will annoy your readers and reduce their confidence in your abilities, damaging your library's reputation.

Even if you are writing content for internal use only, customer service plays a role. Respect the time of your colleagues. Not paying attention to their needs and expectations can harm your professional reputation.

Identifying Your Audience

Your Current Audience

Before you define your message and structure your content, think about the end user: the website visitor, the patron reading his or her email notice, the student trying to navigate signage in the library building, or the colleague trying to interpret your email. Who is on the other end of your content?

For public, external communications, it's useful to identify your primary audience. If you have a marketing or communications office, you may already have defined audiences for particular messages and communication channels. If you have a user-experience department, you may have a similar list of audiences associated with different webpages or other touch points. In an academic library, you might identify first-year students, teaching assistants, and PhD candidates as your main audience segments. In a museum, perhaps your main audiences are out-of-town visitors, researchers, and school groups.

It can be helpful to create personas, if your library doesn't already have some. Personas are fictional characters that represent your audience. When implemented well, you can bring personas into conversations and decision making to ensure you are always keeping the user in mind. At the University of Arizona Libraries, primary personas include:

- Cheyenne, a first-year undergraduate student
- Emily, a graduate student and teaching assistant
- Rahul, a second-year medical student
- Brandon, a PhD candidate
- Renee, a faculty member

You can also identify secondary audiences. These are important audience segments with distinct characteristics, but represent a smaller population. At the University of Arizona Libraries, secondary personas include:

- Elle, a library employee who staffs the service desk
- Craig, a community member who uses library computers
- Donald, a retiree who attends library exhibits and events

If you work in a library, you likely provide content to a similar, diverse group of audience segments. Imagine how your content and messaging might change based on the audience you intend to reach. If your library hasn't yet identified its audience, it is time to do so. And do so intentionally, explicitly, and based on user research.

TIPS FOR PERSONAS

Personas are most useful when you base them on actual user research, such as focus groups, user interviews, surveys, and analytics data. As you put together personas, make them as realistic as possible: give them names, use unique photos of people rather than generic stock photos, and build in actual quotes from your research. Also be sure to include diversity of gender, age, and ethnicity.

With your personas established, identify ways to incorporate them into your project workflows. Consider them whenever you are creating new content or a new service. Bring them up in conversations and let them guide your decision making as you're writing content for a brochure, planning a social media strategy, or putting together a marketing plan for a library service.

Your Potential Audience

You can identify who currently reads your content, but what about who you *want* reading your content? Is there a target market you haven't captured yet, such as potential donors, legislators, or community officials? Maybe there is an untapped audience you would love to reach. Could better content get you there?

Again, a marketing and communications office would probably have an opinion on this topic. It would also be worthwhile to check in with your development officer, director, and strategic planners who might be discussing future directions for your library. You may find value in creating additional personas that represent potential, aspirational audience segments, such as:

- Arch, a potential donor
- Mika, a campus administrator
- Cameron, a student governance leader

While you certainly want to focus on your current audience, don't forget about the untapped potential audience. Thoughtful, focused content can be a powerful and influential tool for reaching those audiences.

Getting to Know Your Readers

Have Empathy

It's important not just to think about your readers, but also to *empathize* with them. An empathetic mind-set is key to user-centered writing. What motivates your readers? What do they struggle with? What are their gaps in knowledge? What would make their lives easier or more enjoyable? Why should they care about what you are writing? What's in it for *them*?

It is your job as a writer to genuinely care about the person on the other end. Practice what Ann Handley calls "pathological empathy." She writes, "Empathy for the customer experience should be at the root of all your content, because having a sense of the people you are writing for and a deep understanding of their problems is key to honing your skill." The most highly skilled content writers are those who observe their users' behaviors, empathize with their challenges, and try to make their lives better. Handley goes on to say, "What matters . . . is creating useful content that solves customer problems, shoulders their burdens, eases their pain, enriches their lives" (2014: 47).

The idea of enriching readers' lives might sound ambitious if you are just writing email responses to customer complaints, but it does speak to the power of good writing. You could write generic, policy-driven responses, or you could write empathetic, human-centered responses. Avoid such cold language as "You are being charged $60 and it is uncontestable. Review section 2.1 of the replacement book policy and pay as soon as possible." Instead, try something more like, "I'm sorry to hear about your car being broken into. I'm sure the last thing you want to worry about is library books. Sadly, we will need to charge you the cost of the books, but let's talk more about payment options and see what we can work out together." Empathetic responses could demonstrate you understand why they are upset, feel their pain, and want to make things right. It's possible that even a short email to a customer could, in fact, make their lives a bit better. Don't underestimate the power of thoughtful writing.

Observe

To better understand your readers, start by observing their behavior. Become an anthropologist of sorts, conducting ethnographic research out in the field. Observe how your readers talk, act, and interact with others. Actively listen to how they describe their successes and challenges. Take mental note of their values and priorities as they make decisions. When you want to know more, ask them questions with a genuine curiosity to learn, understand, and empathize.

Conduct User Research

If you're serious about getting to know your readers, explore more formal research methods. Conduct surveys to get data on demographics, library use, customer feedback, and priorities. Use web analytics tools to see what web content is most popular and how users get to it. Organize focus groups and user interviews to uncover what language people use to describe library services and resources.

As a starting point, compile data that already exists. While libraries serve a diverse audience, you will find common themes. What previous experiences have your readers had with libraries? What is their education level? What do they care about? What keeps them up at night? Notice any gaps in your knowledge, and take the time to fill them in using a variety of methods.

For internal communications, there are a number of things you can do to better understand your colleagues, administrators, and stakeholders. Take a look at job descriptions and CVs to see what background knowledge and experiences people bring to the table. Explore historical documents to see how things have been communicated successfully (or not) in the past. Review any standards of conduct and expectations for communications. Ask your colleagues what methods of communication work best for them. Clarify their needs and expectations. For those colleagues you have the most trouble communicating with, take the time to practice empathy, listen to their concerns, and get to know them on a deeper level.

Identify Your Readers' Levels of Knowledge

Consider the reading level of your audience. Perhaps you can find local data through your community's literacy agencies or published reports. If not, keep in mind that 18 percent of adults (age 16–65) in the United States are at or below the lowest level on the literacy scale (U.S. Department of Education, 2012). This means a significant portion of the population is very limited in reading comprehension. You want to avoid complex sentence structures or vocabulary above the level of your average reader. Especially in public libraries, simple, plain language is your best bet. In fact, plain language is good practice in general, and will be discussed further in chapter 4.

You'll also want to find out what terminology your readers are familiar with. The most misunderstood library terms in usability studies include *catalog*, *periodical*, and *reference* (Kupersmith, 2012). But is this the case regardless of your audience? Perhaps long-standing faculty members or advanced researchers are more familiar with these terms.

But be careful—if you have a broad audience, even familiar terms may have different meanings for different people. Think of the term *database*. Librarians think of databases as subscription-based online portals of articles, books, and other information resources. Software engineers usually think of databases as complex, back-end data systems. Administrative assistants could well think of databases as tables of budget data managed within Microsoft Access. And *database* is just the beginning. Other common library terms that can be misinterpreted include *digital collections*, *digital scholarship*, and *electronic resources*. Do your research and question your assumptions to find out what terminology works best for your audience.

For internal communications, you may have an entirely different set of acceptable vocabulary. Librarians may not bat an eye at *metadata standards*, *ingestion of digital collections*, or *Boolean operators*. But this may not be the case for all library employees. And is it acceptable to use the acronyms *ILS* and *OER*, or do you need to spell out *integrated library system* and *open educational resources*? A little bit of user research can tell you, and will prevent any confusion when you send that email, deliver that report, or present that slideshow.

Beyond terminology, take the time to explore your readers' understanding of broader concepts. Even if they don't know the term *document delivery*, perhaps they are familiar with the service of requesting articles. Maybe they don't know the term *express retrieval*, but they understand that the library will pull books and place them on the hold shelf. On the other hand, some concepts could be entirely mysterious to them. Perhaps it's not just the term *subject guide* that is unfamiliar, but so is the entire notion of a research guide on a particular topic.

Again, your internal audience will have different levels of knowledge than your external audience. Librarians might understand the concept of link resolvers for accessing content, or mapping catalog metadata into a discovery tool, whereas your average library visitor would not be able to easily conceptualize either of these things.

So when identifying the knowledge level of your audience, ask the following:

- What is their reading level?
- What is their background knowledge and experience?
- What terminology are they familiar with?
- What acronyms need to be spelled out?
- What concepts are they familiar with?

Knowing what your readers already know or don't know will help you focus your writing. It will allow you to remove unnecessary or redundant content while expanding upon or simplifying something that might be a new topic for most readers.

Identify Your Readers' Goals

With an understanding of who you are writing for, you can then determine their goals—the utility of your content. What's in it for them? Ask:

- What do your readers need?
- What do they expect?
- What do they want to learn?
- What do they want to experience?

- How do they want to feel?
- What do they want to do?

Your content can serve a variety of user goals. In chapter 3 you will learn more about defining content goals and purpose, but it's important to start thinking about them at the outset as you analyze your audience. How does your content help your readers? Perhaps it helps them:

- Complete a task
- Solve a problem
- Make a decision
- Save time
- Get inspired
- Be entertained
- Learn something new

Identify Your Readers' Challenges and Motivations

To write with your audience in mind, become familiar with their challenges and motivations. For example, imagine you are writing a webpage about book delivery for an online student audience. You know that they tend to be returning students who work full time and do their coursework in the evenings and weekends. So in general, your readers are going to:

- Have demanding schedules, juggling school, work, and personal commitments
- Be highly motivated to be successful in their coursework to improve their professional opportunities

With this in mind, you can make it clear on the webpage that this book delivery service will address some of their challenges: it will save them time and effort. You can address their motivations, too: it will make them more successful in their class projects. Framing your content this way will make it more relevant and meaningful to your readers.

Identify Your Readers' Context

A reader sitting down to enjoy an article on a topic that is important to her is in a different frame of mind than someone who is trying to quickly read a terms of use statement on a website. Think about your reader's environment and mental state. Think about her context. Ask:

- How is she finding it?
  - Did she actively seek out the content?
  - Did the content unexpectedly show up in her mail or email?
- What brought her to that point?
  - Is this her first attempt to find the answer to her question?
  - How motivated is she to read it?
- What does she want to do next?
  - Does she want to save or share your content?
  - Is there a task or call to action this content will help her with?

- What is her mood and frame of mind?
  - Is she frustrated or relaxed?
  - Is she under time constraints?
  - What is her level of patience?
- If it's digital content, what device is she using to access it?
  - Is it a handheld, laptop, or desktop computer?
  - Is it a touchscreen device?
- What might distract her away from your content?
  - Is she reading this on her lunch break?
  - Is she on the bus or in a work meeting?
- How does this content fit into other aspects of her life?
  - Is reading your content part of her regular routine?
  - Does your content compete with similar content?
- How will she approach your content?
  - Will she read it all in one sitting, or come back to it later?
  - Will she read it word-for-word, or skim it to find the information she needs?

These are a lot of questions, but they are important. By understanding your readers' context, you can frame your message in the most effective way.

Things All Readers Have in Common

Readers Are Busy

While getting to know your own particular audience is important, you can make some pretty safe assumptions. For one, they are in a rush and easily distracted. And even if they are not, writing with the busy reader in mind will only improve your writing. It will encourage you to focus and simplify your message. As Natalie Canavor writes, "Write for the overscheduled, information-loaded, low attention span, impatient, and skeptical audience—which is all of them" (2016: 8).

Readers Are Self-Interested

You can also count on your readers to care about their own interests. It's a natural human trait: humans want to know "what's in it for me," often referred to as the WIIFM principle in business writing. Always be sure to speak to your readers' motivations and interests.

Key Points

Good writing starts with a good understanding of your audience. Remember:

- Practice empathy, keeping your readers in the forefront of your mind.
- Test your assumptions and get to know your readers in a variety of ways.
- Pay attention to your readers' knowledge, goals, and context.
- No matter your audience, it's good practice to write for the busy, self-interested reader.

Now that you have a sense of who you're writing for, it's time to think about the message and purpose of your writing. In chapter 3, you'll identify your content goals, structure, voice, and tone.

⑥ References

Canavor, Natalie. 2016. *Business Writing Today: A Practical Guide.* Los Angeles: Sage Publications.

Handley, Ann. 2014. *Everybody Writes: Your Go-To Guide for Creating Ridiculously Good Content.* Hoboken, NJ: Wiley.

King, Stephen. 2000. *On Writing: A Memoir of the Craft.* New York: Scribner.

Kupersmith, John. 2012. "Library Terms That Users Understand." *LAUC-B and Library Staff Research.* eScholarship. University of California. https://escholarship.org/uc/item/3qq499w7.

Ross, Catherine, and Kirsti Nilsen. 2013. *Communicating Professionally.* 3rd ed. Chicago: Neal-Schuman.

U.S. Department of Education, National Center for Education Statistics. 2012. *Literacy, Numeracy, and Problem Solving in Technology-Rich Environments among U.S. Adults: Results from the Program for the International Assessment of Adult Competencies 2012.* http://nces.ed.gov/pubs2014/2014008.pdf.

Defining Your Message and Purpose

▷ How to balance user goals with organizational goals

▷ How to define the purpose of your writing, including any call(s) to action

▷ Ways to prioritize and structure your writing based on your message

MOST HARD-TO-UNDERSTAND WRITING lacks a clear purpose or structure. This is why it is important to consider your message and purpose at the outset. In this chapter, you will determine the purpose of what you are writing, taking into account the readers' goals and expectations as well as what you would like readers to actually *do* with the information provided. You will then bring structure to your written content, prioritizing the most essential messages and organizing it in a way that makes sense to the reader.

Identifying User Needs and Goals

Writing for the user experience is key. Understand your audience, or your writing is doomed for failure. How to get to know your readers is covered in chapter 2. Let's assume at this point that you have a firm grasp of your readers' needs, expectations, and habits. Now you are at the point of putting pen to paper (or fingers to keyboard). How do you use this information to create better content?

How People Really Read

Most of the time, readers are skimming your content rather than reading it word for word. It's true that as much thought as you put into the selection and placement of each word on a page, most of your readers aren't going to be consuming it in this traditional, linear fashion. Even in a full-length book format, such as this, there is a good chance that you, as the reader, are doing more skimming than reading. Am I right?

Readers skim. This has long been an accepted fact for digital content: 28 percent of words on a webpage get read by the page visitor, and probably less than that (Nielsen, 2008). Even in academic settings, students and faculty alike are now used to "minimalist" reading, the "power browse," or the "snippet" approach to digital text (Baron, 2015). There is ongoing research related to the difference in consumption of digital and print media, but one study found that there was no significant difference between the levels of comprehension for print and digital presentation of content (Sun, Shieh, and Huang, 2013). The line between digital and print is becoming fuzzier. With the introduction of electronic readers aimed to look more like print, such as the Kindle, and the constant evolution of technology for reading and interacting with text, it is a pretty safe assumption that readers are often skimming your content regardless of format.

So whether it is an email, a flyer, or a webpage, it's rare for somebody to sit down and read the content continuously, word for word, line by line. (An exception to this is fiction or creative writing, which is a whole different topic requiring a whole different approach. This book doesn't intend to cover that topic—there are many other books, and more appropriate authors, to write on that topic.)

What Readers Want

It goes without saying that readers want content to be understandable and easy to navigate, but what else do they want? The way you go about writing should vary greatly depending on your readers' mind-sets, intentions, and expectations.

Some types of writing are for entertainment. Perhaps you have a staff-curated blog that teaches readers about interesting items in your collection. Maybe you have reviews of books or documentaries, or compelling stories about members of your community. A good way to frame user needs is through personas, as discussed in chapter 2. To frame the expectations of your reader for this type of content, you might say, "Donald wants to: (1) be entertained, (2) get inspired, and (3) discover something new."

More common scenarios in libraries are when the user wants to learn something. Maybe you are writing a brochure on library services for students. In this case, you might say, "Cheyenne wants to: (1) know how many books she can check out, (2) find out the locations of the different libraries, and (3) discover what technology she can borrow from the library."

By identifying your user needs and articulating them, you will have an outline of what content you need to cover. Be careful to limit the number of user goals you are trying to meet in just a single piece of content. If you find yourself with a list of a dozen or more goals, consider more than one content approach (e.g., multiple webpages, a news story and a webpage, both text and video). You also will need to prioritize what comes when, which is discussed later in this chapter.

As you think through the intention of your content, frame it in the eyes of your readers, appealing to their goals and mind-sets. As Ann Handley explains, "Reframe the idea to relate it to your readers. Why does it matter to them? What is in it for them? Why should they care? What's the clear lesson or message you want them to take away? What value do you offer them? What questions might they have? What advice or help can you provide?" (2014: 28).

⌖ Identifying Organizational Purpose and Goals

Sometimes, the user needs will clearly align with your organizational goals, but not always. What are your personal or organizational goals, and how do they fit in with the context of your users' goals? Oftentimes, you want to do something for your readers in order to reach a related organizational goal. For instance, your intention could be to:

- Inform readers of your circulation policies so that they don't get late fees.
- Entertain readers so that they like the library and support it down the road.
- Tell your story so that readers can advocate for the library within the community.

There are a variety of things your writing could be intended to do. What are your goals and purpose? Do you intend to:

- Inform?
- Entertain?
- Provoke?
- Entice?
- Excite?
- Convince?
- Persuade?

Perhaps you want to actually sell something to your users, such as library-published books or a fee-based service (e.g., journal publishing, 3D printing). Or maybe you want to get buy-in for something your library is doing. In times of limited budgets and staffing, it is as important as ever to have a community supporting the work that you do. Or maybe you are trying to get someone to try a new service or attend an upcoming event—even if it's a free service or opportunity, you still have to convince them it is worth their time and effort. In all of these cases, you need to ask yourself, "What's in it for them?" You need to make sure your content addresses this question directly to be most effective.

Similar to your user needs and goals, you don't want to have a lot of organizational goals here. The more goals you identify, the harder it is to convey your content in a way that is understandable to the reader. Your most important goals can get lost in a sea of content. So don't try to do too much. Focusing is key.

Also important is to make sure your content goals align with the broader strategic goals of your library. For example, if you are hosting a lecture on a topic of strategic importance to the library, present the content in a way that reflects this. In promotional materials, the basic content would just be, "Will Simpson presents on the Future of Scholarly Publishing, Main Library, Thursday, April 30." This type of content has no voice or real message behind it. To better align the messaging with the broader strategic goal of your library, you could instead write, "Join the library as we lead discussions on the future of scholarly publishing. Hear invited guest Will Simpson. . . ." Pay attention to these types of opportunities to communicate your strategic goals and directions as a library in your public-facing content.

Defining Your Primary Messages and Calls to Action

Define Your Primary Messages

Your primary messages are the core points you are trying to make in your content. Brainstorm a list of messages based on your user and organizational goals. Then ruthlessly refine your list until you're left with only the essentials. In many cases, this will be just one or two things. For example, your primary messages for a webpage on e-books could be:

- Use this search box to find all e-books in the library.
- Alternatively, go to a specific e-book provider to browse their collection by topic.

If you are creating a brochure for Friends of the Library, your primary messages could be:

- The library does amazing things for the community.
- It only costs $50 to become an annual friend and get all sorts of benefits.

Define Your Calls to Action

In web design, a "call to action" is the thing you want the user to do next. This concept can apply to writing in any format. If you intend for the reader to *do* something with the information, you have a call to action. Do you want the reader to respond in some way, take a next step, or complete some other action? Calls to action might be:

- Search for e-books.
- Become a Friend of the Library.
- Request a book through interlibrary loan.
- Request the library purchase a book.
- Sign up for the library newsletter.
- Like the library on Facebook.

On webpages and in emails, there is usually some call to action. As you think about how to structure your content, the call to action is perhaps the most important consideration of all. In fact, if there is not a call to action, you may want to reconsider the goals of the content and if the content is even necessary.

The call to action answers the reader's question: what now? Even if the answer is something boring like "go back to the other document," that should be clear. If you don't have a call to action in mind, again go back to thinking of the user. What might he or she want to do next? See related content? Read more? Contact a person? Make a comment? By thinking through what the reader might want to do next, you might realize that there is actually a call to action you hadn't yet considered.

IS THERE ALWAYS A CALL TO ACTION?

Not always. Especially in content that libraries provide, sometimes the purpose is for the reader to absorb the information and then move on to something else. Perhaps the goal is for the person to simply read and understand the content, but by doing this they will then do something outside in the world. They will be armed with newfound knowledge and will be able to put it to good use. Perhaps you have an informational webpage about scholarly publishing or copyright. A call to action could be to contact a librarian or to sign a petition or make some kind of request, but it could also simply be for them to become more informed and use the information in their future studies or research. This is okay, and while it is not a traditional call to action, it is still something that you, as a writer, need to think about as you write and structure your content. Just always consider: what do you want them to *learn*, and then what do you want them to *do*?

Prioritizing and Structuring Content

Step Back

Now that you have a good understanding of your users' and organization's goals, as well as your primary messages and any calls to action, you should have some sense of what content is required. What is the breadth and depth of content needed to accomplish these goals? You may realize at this point that what you thought would be a simple webpage should actually be more than that: several webpages, a news story, and a blog post. On the other hand, you may find that while you had initially intended something to be an entire section on your website, it could be a shorter-lived news story instead.

Put Key Messages First

With goals and messages in hand, it is time to prioritize your content. Of everything, what is most important? If your primary purpose is to convince or persuade the reader, then your key message is likely explaining what is in it for them. Why should they care?

In high school or even college-level English composition classes, you may have been taught the traditional essay structure: introduction, body, conclusion. This narrative, chronological approach forces the reader to get all the way to the end before learning the main point. Many writing instructors have gotten away from this format because it doesn't work well in the real world. It doesn't appeal to the browsing and skimming nature of today's busy reader. Think about such documents as a grant application, a project report, or a project update. Do you want to hear the entire background and history before the "meat" of the thing? No, you want to hear about the update first. You want what is most important and relevant, and you want it now.

In journalism, writers are taught to organize their writing in the form of an "inverted pyramid." This means their primary messages come first, since many readers skim the headlines and first sentences of news and other informational content. This also applies to much of our writing as librarians. Whether it is in an email, on a webpage, or in a document, your most important message should come first, almost always.

The title is often where the key message—or at least part of it—should go, whether it is the title of a brochure, the title of a webpage, or the subject line of an email. If you can break down the content to one key message, what would it be? Make sure that your message is speaking in the language of your audience. How will this content help them reach their goals? Key, actionable messages are reflected in titles such as:

- Search for e-Books
- Become a Friend of the Library
- Apply for a Study Room

More complete messages, reflected in the body or headers of the content, could be along the lines of:

- Search for e-books in one easy search box.
- Become a Friend of the Library and help us be the best we can be.
- Apply for a long-term study room and get the quiet space you need.

As Ginny Redish explains in her influential book on web writing, *Letting Go of the Words*, "Whatever your key message is, put it first. Put it in the headline (the bite) and elaborate it quickly in the beginning of the text (the snack)" (2012: 136).

Put Calls to Action in Obvious Places

When you have a call to action, this should be apparent to the reader from skimming the text. An all-too-common mistake in writing is to place a call to action deep within a paragraph, forcing the reader to skim through a lot of text to find the link they are looking for. As demonstrated table 3.1, simply placing the call to action at the beginning of a sentence can make it more prominent to the user and indicate its importance.

Table 3.1. Placement of Call to Action

LESS OBVIOUS CALL TO ACTION	MORE PROMINENT CALL TO ACTION
Our archive has unique collections from the southwest, borderlands, and the university. The best way to browse our collections is to see our *collections by subject*.	*Collections by subject* are the best way to browse our archive's unique collections from the southwest, borderlands, and the university.

Create an Overall Structure

In future chapters, you will learn some of the tools for organizing and structuring your content, such as headings, links, and bulleted lists. For now, just think about how you might structure your content based on priority. As mentioned earlier, you should probably put the most important information first, and supplemental information last.

What order and structure will help you best communicate your primary messages? Ginny Redish (2012) suggests you break up your content into discrete topics and subtopics. You can break these topics up by time or sequence, task, people, type of information, or questions people ask. See table 3.2 for possible ways to order different types of content.

Table 3.2. Ways to Order Content

TYPE OF CONTENT	POSSIBLE WAY TO ORDER
Instructions	Chronologically
Search options	By task (e.g., search for an article, a book, or a film)
Circulation privileges	By audience type (e.g., student, faculty member, community member)
List of databases	Alphabetically
Form	By type of information
Frequently asked questions	By order users might ask them

Ross and Nilsen provide even more ordering options—by spatial sequence, attributes of comparison, or pro and con (2013). If you are writing about study rooms, ordering by each floor could work well. If you are writing a report comparing database options, you might organize your content by first comparing cost, then content, then usability of the different products. If you are preparing a report outlining a new travel policy, readers might appreciate reading a list of benefits first followed by a list of drawbacks.

CAUTION ON ORGANIZING BY AUDIENCE

When breaking up your content by audience, be careful that you aren't excluding anyone. If you have a website section "For Faculty" and "For Graduate Students," but you don't have a section "For Undergraduate Students," your undergraduate students may feel left out and unwelcome.

Again, remember your audience. How would they approach this content? Thinking about the content from their perspective can help guide your organization. When in doubt, try one approach, gather feedback, and evaluate if your approach works well or if you need to adjust it. (Learn more about evaluating and revising content in chapter 14.)

As you think about overall structure, also identify opportunities to layer information. Rather than providing all information in a single email, webpage, or document, can you link out to details in some areas, or have details collapsed, with the option to expand? On a website, you can have brief descriptions of your databases displayed along with a clickable icon that allows users to see more details. In a document, you can link out to associated documents rather than quoting them in full, or use footnotes or endnotes if there is information useful to some, but not all, of your readers. Layering information in this way makes content less overwhelming and more focused, as well as giving users control over their own experience.

◎ Key Points

Identifying your goals and the goals of your readers, and then structuring content to meet those goals, is core to the writing process. How you apply these steps in your own writing will vary based on the context. An email to a colleague will obviously require less analysis than a ten-page report you plan to deliver next month to the library advisory board. Whatever the scale, though, these concepts set a foundation for useful content. Remember:

- Let user and organizational needs guide your primary messages.
- Put the most important content front and center.
- Prioritize and structure content based on its purpose.

Now that you have identified your messages and goals, it is time to get to work on the particulars of effective content. In the next chapter, you will learn ways to simplify your writing.

References

Baron, Naomi. 2015. "The Plague of tl;dr." *The Chronicle Review*, February 9. http://chronicle.com/article/The-Plague-of-tl-dr/151635.

Handley, Ann. 2014. *Everybody Writes*. Hoboken, NJ: John Wiley & Sons.

Nielsen, Jakob. 2008. "How Little Do Users Read?" Nielsen Norman Group. May 6. www.nngroup.com/articles/how-little-do-users-read.

Redish, Janice (Ginny). 2012. *Letting Go of the Words: Writing Web Content that Works*. 2nd ed. Waltham, MA: Morgan Kaufmann.

Ross, Catherine, and Kirsti Nilsen. *Communicating Professionally*. 3rd ed. Chicago: Neal-Schuman, 2013.

Szu-Yuan Sun, Chich-Jen Shieh, and Kai-Ping Huang. 2013. "A Research on Comprehension Differences between Print and Screen Reading." *South African Journal of Economic and Management Sciences* 16, no. 5: 87–101.

Keeping It Simple

WHILE CHALLENGING, clarity in your writing is essential. People are more likely to read the content and process your message. In this chapter, you will learn why writing in plain, succinct language is so important, and how to go about doing it.

Brevity Matters

Strengthen Your Message

A classic guide, *The Elements of Style*, provided a foundational rule for writers: omit needless words. The authors proclaim, "A sentence should contain no unnecessary words, a paragraph no unnecessary sentences, for the same reason that a drawing should have no unnecessary lines and a machine no unnecessary parts" (Strunk and White, 1999: 25).

Redundancies, jargon, and complex constructions all contribute to cluttered content, the "disease" of American writing (Zinsser, 2006: 6). Highlight and strengthen your message by stripping down your writing to its cleanest, most vital components.

Save the Time of the Reader

With librarianship comes a culture of educating users. Sadly, this well-meaning approach supports a tendency to overshare information, leading to cumbersome, text-heavy content that frustrates readers. At odds with this culture is one of Ranganathan's five laws of library science: save the time of the reader. Librarians need to strike a balance between providing substantive content while also keeping it understandable and efficient. Respect your readers' time and cognitive load through crisp, purposeful language.

Use Plain Language

Plain language, or *plain English*, refers to content that people can easily read, understand, and use (Horton and Quesenbery, 2013). Since the 1990s, the U.S. government has mandated that governmental communications follow plain language guidelines. The philosophy is that citizens deserve clear communications from their government. They should be able to find what they need, understand what they find, and use what they find to meet their needs (PlainLanguage.gov, 2015). So plain language is not only good practice but also the law if you are working in a library supported by government funding.

Simplify, Don't Dumb Down

When you tell others you want to simplify things, they might assert you are just "dumbing things down." But writing well is not about dumbing it down. It's about considering, respecting, and having empathy for the reader. As Ann Handley writes, "No one will ever complain that you've made things too simple to understand. Of course, simple does not equal dumbed down. . . . *Assume the reader knows nothing. But don't assume the reader is stupid.*" (2014: 72).

It Is Worth the Effort

Writing in a simple, understandable format can be challenging. Ironically, it takes more thought, organization, and revision to write something succinct than it does to write a couple of paragraphs that say the same thing. But it's worth the effort. Allocate extra time to your next writing project. And even if you can't tackle all your existing content anytime soon, Kimble insists that you can at least get started and "pick off some of the prime offenders" (2012: 27).

WRITING AND THINKING

Writing is a mental activity, so focused thought leads to focused writing. If you are feeling cluttered mentally, it will be reflected on the page. Practice self-awareness, mindfulness, and reflection. If your writing is sloppy, you might need to step back and regain your concentration. Meditate, exercise, or do something else that helps you focus your energy and train of thought.

Simplifying Paragraphs

Keep Paragraphs Short

White space is easier on the eyes and makes content easier to skim and digest, so aim for short paragraphs. Zinsser explains that "short paragraphs put air around what you write and make it look inviting, whereas a long chunk of type can discourage a reader from even starting to read" (2006: 78). Natalie Canavor echoes this sentiment, arguing that shorter paragraphs are more likely to gain your readers' interest, keep your readers with you, and make the content easier to grasp (2016).

Canavor advocates for three to five sentences per paragraph (2016), and Handley takes it further and recommends no more than three sentences or six lines (2014). And unless you're writing a book or scholarly article, it's usually okay to have a paragraph with just one sentence. (In this chapter, there is an average of 3.3 sentences per paragraph.)

> ### BE INTENTIONAL WITH PARAGRAPH BREAKS
>
> While you should keep paragraphs to just a few sentences, be purposeful about it. Don't break up content arbitrarily just to follow the short-paragraph rule. Paragraphs serve to create a logical structure and should help readers understand the flow and purpose of the content.

Hide Less Relevant Content

As you organize your content, consider having supplementary content hidden at first. This can be a useful way to keep paragraphs simple and to the point, giving the reader control if they desire to read more. You can accomplish this in print using footnotes, endnotes, or asterisks, or digitally using an expand-or-collapse option.

While useful, this technique can be done well and can be done poorly. Keep in mind your users' goals and behaviors as well as your voice and tone. Key messages need to be prominent. Using footnotes and endnotes may come across as too formal. If you have an asterisk on a brochure, that's fine, but make sure the asterisk is actually defined somewhere. Seeing an asterisk but no definition of what it means is a frustrating experience for the reader. So if you use this technique, be thoughtful and strategic about it.

⑥ Simplifying Sentences

Keep Sentences Short

Sentences need to be easily digestible. Natalie Canavor (2016) recommends an average of fourteen to eighteen words per sentence (with some shorter and some longer). Ann Handley (2014) recommends no more than twenty-five words in a sentence. (In this chapter, the average number of words per sentences is 12.4.)

The words within your sentences make a difference, so pay attention to the complexity of the words and how they work together. Read your sentences out loud to see if they are hard to follow. If you find yourself questioning whether a sentence is too long, it probably is.

Break apart complex content. Notice if you have explanatory details set off by parentheses or dashes. Are the details necessary, or are they superfluous? If you can't make a long sentence shorter without losing meaning, make it more than one sentence. If you have a significant message placed in parentheses mid-sentence, take it out and put it in another sentence. In cases where you can't avoid writing a long sentence, at least make sure it's under control from beginning to end and that readers can easily follow along (Zinsser, 2006).

Remove Unnecessary Adverbs

Watch out for adverbs that serve no value. Unless your adverb changes the meaning of the sentence, see if you can do without it. Try to use better verbs or adjectives to convey the same message in a bold, succinct way.

Not only can adverbs make sentences longer than they should be, but they can also make your writing passive or redundant. Stephen King is pretty passionate about this point, contending not only that "the adverb is not your friend" (2000: 124) but also that "the road to hell is paved with adverbs, and I will shout it from the rooftops" (2000: 125). He is being facetious, of course, but it is a strong word of caution. While adverbs can serve a purpose, they are overused. Table 4.1 has some basic examples of how a single word can better convey a message than an adverb phrase.

Table 4.1. Strong Words Replacing Adverb Phrases

ORIGINAL ADVERB PHRASE	REVISED
Very small	Tiny
Very large	Huge
Extremely sad	Devastated
Argue strongly	Insist
Decrease significantly	Dwindle
Grow exponentially	Skyrocket

Remove Meaningless Modifiers

Be careful about other words and phrases that intend to provide context or detail, but ultimately serve no purpose. You will often see meaningless modifiers at the beginning of sentences. Take, for example:

- Please note. . . .
- It should be noted that. . . .
- It is interesting to note that. . . .
- It is suggested that. . . .
- I should point out that. . . .
- The fact that. . . .
- You will find that. . . .

Most of the time, you can simply remove these modifiers. Including them on occasion to help with the flow of your content is fine, but be cautious of using these when they don't add meaning. Be especially cautious if you find yourself using a lot of them.

There are also small, one- or two-word modifiers that serve little purpose. Examples of needless modifiers include *sort of*, *a bit*, *rather*, *somewhat*, and *quite*. These carry some meaning, but not much. They can also hurt your voice, since they make you sound timid or unsure of yourself. If you see these qualifiers in a sentence, ask yourself if they contribute meaning. If they don't, remove them.

Remove Redundant Adjectives

Often, adjectives are also overused or used poorly. For example, consider the sentence: "The library's strategic plan is innovative, creative, and forward-thinking." Rather than listing three comparable adjectives, pick your favorite one that best reflects what you are trying to say. Or better yet, find words that capture the spirit of the lot, giving you something like, "The library's strategic plan is breaking new ground." This revision creates a bolder sentence. It cuts to the chase and removes redundancies.

Too often, writers get stuck on the power of three and insist on using three adjectives to describe something. If you find yourself trying to add one more adjective, stop for a moment and reconsider. Is another adjective really needed? What words *best describe* the message you are trying to get across?

Remove Pointless Imperatives

When writing directional content, watch out for unnecessary imperatives at the beginning of your sentences. These usually serve no purpose and distract from your intention. For example:

- Please go to the information desk. . . .
- Be sure to fill out the online form. . . .
- You may want to contact us with questions. . . .
- Don't forget to renew your print card. . . .

These can be better written as just:

- Go to the information desk.
- Fill out the online form.
- Contact us with questions.
- Renew your print card.

Remove Boring Transitions

While often useful and sometimes essential to creating flow between content, transitions are often overused. Unless writing a long-form document and the relationship between content is unclear, you can probably do without these at the beginning of a sentence:

- Also
- In addition
- Additionally
- Furthermore
- Along similar lines

- At the same time
- As such

That said, transitions can be useful to alert the reader you are switching gears. If a transition is necessary to alter your tone or change the reader's orientation, by all means use one. But try to pick more meaningful transition language. If you are changing moods or perspectives, try words such as:

- But
- Yet
- Still
- That said

If you are changing orientations, use words like:

- Now
- Later
- After
- Earlier

Replace Extraneous Prepositions

Watch out for overuse of prepositions—those words that place other words in a time, place, or context. Prepositions, including *of*, *to*, *in*, and *by*, can lead to wordy sentences when you have too many of them (Canavor, 2016). Rather than writing, "Our librarians *in the* technology unit can advise you how to use 3D printing *to the* maximum degree," try, "Our technology unit's librarians can advise you how to best use 3D printing." And Kimble recommends taking special aim at multiword prepositions, such as *prior to*, *with regard to*, and *in connection with* (2012: 9). It's best to avoid these altogether.

Remove Phony Niceties

Librarians are a polite bunch, which often means using *please*, *thank you*, and *sorry* all over the place. Nine times out of ten, these friendly words serve little purpose. Use them thoughtfully and when you actually mean it. Don't arbitrarily put them at the beginning and ends of your sentences. For example, you can remove the niceties from the following sentences:

- ~~Please~~ return your books to the book drop during open hours. ~~Thank you~~.
- ~~Please~~ return this item as soon as possible to avoid the replacement fee.
- The main branch will be closed today for a special event. ~~Thank you~~.
- ~~We're sorry for the trouble, but~~ we ask that you ~~please~~ don't let others use your library card.

When these niceties *are* appropriate is when you recognize that you are frustrating your users or they enhance your voice and tone. These words can convey that you care and are genuinely thankful to them or apologetic about something. For example:

- We are experiencing intermittent problems accessing MyAccount and are working on a solution. Thank you for your patience.
- The library will close at 5 p.m. due to the holiday. We are sorry for the inconvenience.

⑥ Simplifying Phrases and Words

Choose the Right Words

Be deliberate in your word choice. Short, familiar words are usually your best bet. Longer, less conventional words can annoy your readers and even make them skeptical. There are a lot of words in the English language, but Natalie Canavor recommends, "Use the one- and two-syllable words as much as you can and consciously use the longer words when you need them because a shorter word won't work or you want the effect" (2016: 69).

Avoid or Explain Jargon

Beware of library speak and other jargon—terminology your readers won't understand or appreciate. You run the risk of not just sounding too formal, but also sounding pretentious, unapproachable, or phony. If your audience includes nonnative speakers, they will have an especially hard time understanding any jargon.

In the cases where it is appropriate to use jargon, do so thoughtfully for a specific purpose. For example, you might be educating users on a topic as part of an instructional webpage or tutorial.

You might be surprised to discover the breadth of terms unfamiliar to average library users. John Kupersmith compiled data found in fifty-one usability studies and confirmed that terminology is frequently the culprit (Kupersmith, 2012). Common library terms to watch out for include:

- Catalog, OPAC, databases, database providers, discovery tools
- Call numbers, SuDocs, accession numbers
- Circulation, circulating, noncirculating, loan period
- Collections, digital collections, special collections
- E-audio, e-journals, e-resources, electronic resources
- Information commons, learning commons
- Information literacy, information fluency
- Interlibrary loan, document delivery, recall
- Link resolvers, OpenURL
- Metadata, subject headings, facets
- Periodicals, serials, monographs
- Reference, reference assistance, reference resources
- Repository, institutional repository, digital preservation
- Scholarly communication, digital scholarship, alternative publishing
- Open access, open educational resources
- Search expressions, Boolean operators, wildcards, truncation
- Subject guides, course guides, research guides, pathfinders

Avoid Buzzwords and Other Silly Words

Buzzwords, corporate speak, and fancy vocabulary can be equally problematic. Buzzwords are overused, carry little meaning, and tend to sound pretty silly. Corporate speak and highbrow vocabulary is annoying to read and sounds less human. Try to stay clear of such words as:

- Affiliates
- Considerations
- Hereby, therein, wherefore
- Implementation
- Incentivize
- Innovative, innovate, innovation
- Learnings
- Leverage, optimize, maximize
- Milieu
- Solutions (when referring to things like "printing solutions")
- Strategic, strategize, strategy
- Synergy, synergize, synergies

Use Concise, Specific Words

Leave no room for ambiguity. The reader should not have to pause to question what something means, so follow the sixteenth rule in *The Elements of Style*: use definite, specific, concrete language. As you select each word on the page, "prefer the specific to the general, the definite to the vague, the concrete to the abstract" (Strunk and White, 1999: 30).

Watch out for commonly used library words that carry little meaning, such as *services* and *resources*. Instead, convey clarity with words like *study rooms* and *books*.

Many popular words and phrases can be replaced with a simpler variation, as shown in table 4.2. These revisions don't hinder meaning; they just make the content easier to digest. Some credit for this list goes to Ann Handley, who has her own excellent list of overused words and their simplified equivalents (2014: 103–4). If you like this kind of thing, you can even download a thirty-five-page list of alternative words produced by the United Kingdom government (Plain English Campaign, 2016).

Avoid Repetition

Canavor (2016) warns against placing similarly constructed words near each other, particularly words ending in *-ion*, *-ing*, *-ity*, and *-ed*. It's irritating to read the sentence "The crea*tion* of the administra*tion* office is due to the reorganiza*tion*" or "We are question*ing* the reason*ing* behind the choos*ing* of this software." To prevent this issue, include no more than one *-ion*, one *-ing*, one *-ity*, and one *-ed* word per sentence. Using active voice and present tense will help, too.

Along the same lines, watch out for too many words ending in *-ly* or *-y*, indicating you have too many adverbs and/or adjectives. And be careful not to include more than one *by* in a sentence, as in "The presentation by the speaker received rave reviews by the audience." Or too many instances of *the*, *and*, or *or*. In fact, any time you have too many instances of any word, you may have a readability problem.

Table 4.2. Simplified Phrases and Words

ORIGINAL	REVISED
Utilize, leverage	Use
To ensure	For
In order to	To
With the possible exception of	Except for
Whenever, at which time	When
At this point in time, immediately	Now, today
At the same time	Meanwhile
Continues to be	Remains, is
Remainder of time	Rest of time
There are times when	Sometimes, at times
At the end of the day	Ultimately
Numerous, a number of	Many, several, some
Lengthy	Long
The majority of	Most
Initial	First
Referred to as	Called
The reason why is that	Because
In spite of	Despite
In spite of the fact that, despite the fact that	Although, though
Ways by which	Ways

Test the Readability of Your Content

A great way to test the understandability of your content is to have people read it and provide feedback. Start by reading it aloud to yourself—does it make sense? Then ask people in your audience to read it and convey back to you what they thought it meant. Ask them specific questions to find out if your messages came through as intended.

While the human reading experience is the only authentic measure of readability, there is also technology and math to help. You evaluate the readability of your content by using one of several readability scales. Flesch-Kincaid readability testing, first developed in the 1970s, looks at word length, sentence length, and number of syllables. The lower your score on the Flesch Reading Ease test, the less readable your writing is. Other established readability indexes include the automated readability index (ARI), Gunning-Fog index, SMOG index, Fry readability formula, and Coleman-Liau index.

Microsoft Word, perhaps the most common text editor in the world, comes with a built-in readability test. You can also use free web-based tools, such as readability-score.

com, and free downloads, such as Readability™ for iTunes and Google Chrome, to evaluate content. Or if you are a do-it-yourselfer, you can always calculate your scores manually.

When writing for a general audience, you want to aim for a grade level of 7 or 8 across the different scales. A score of 10–12 is roughly the reading level on completion of high school, so this is acceptable if you are writing for a college-level audience. But keep in mind that the average American reads at a seventh-grade level (Canavor, 2016: 67).

To give you an idea of what this looks like, this book chapter scores a grade of about 7.3 on Flesch-Kincaid, 10.3 on Gunning-Fog, and 13.4 on Coleman-Liau. It is expected that content will score differently depending on the index, since what is being measured is different. For example, the score is higher for Coleman-Liau than it is for Flesch-Kincaid because it evaluates on characters instead of syllables per word. To lower a Coleman-Liau score, you'd need to reduce the number of words with a high number of characters.

So while they aren't the only way to evaluate your content, get in the habit of checking readability scores. If you score grade level 12 or higher, try simplifying your content, reducing the number of syllables, characters, and words per sentence.

⊚ Cut, Cut, and Cut Again

Even when you think your writing is clear, you can probably cut more. Pay attention to tiny words and superfluous details. There is almost always something else that can be removed.

As you continue to simplify, remember your content goals. Every paragraph, sentence, and word—every morsel of content—should serve a purpose. If any part of it doesn't meet either your goals or your users' goals, it's probably safe to go ahead and remove it.

For inspiration, see the examples in table 4.3. These are sentences that have been revised from their original versions. They could probably be simplified even further.

Table 4.3. Simplified Sentences

ORIGINAL SENTENCE	REVISED SENTENCE
The branch library closed for a full renovation starting Monday, October 15, 2015, and the renovation is expected to be completed in December 2017.	The branch library is closed for renovation from October 15, 2015, until December 2017.
Due to the severe weather conditions in the surrounding area, all units of the New York Public Library will be CLOSED today, Wednesday February 10, 2016.	Due to severe weather, all of NYPL will be closed today, Wednesday, February 10, 2016.
Whenever possible, the library will provide a version with English captions to ensure ADA compliance.	When possible, we provide a version with English captions for ADA compliance.
Questions and comments regarding interlibrary loan policies and procedures may be directed to ill@email.edu.	Contact us about interlibrary loan at ill@email.edu.
The Espresso Book Machine (EBM) is an on-demand book maker that will print and bind your book in minutes. The EBM will provide you with a library-quality paperback copy.	We can print and bind your book in minutes with our Espresso Book Machine. This on-demand book maker creates a library-quality paperback.
There are certain types of materials that only circulate for a specific period of time.	Some materials can only be borrowed for a specific period of time.

🌀 Key Points

Writing concisely respects your readers' time and ensures your message is front and center. Remember:

- Keep paragraphs and sentences succinct.
- Choose words that are unambiguous and easy to understand.
- Make sure every word on the page serves a purpose.
- You can almost always cut a bit more.

Now that you've learned techniques for keeping things simple, it is time to expand upon language choice. In the next chapter, you'll learn how to use an active, conversational style in all your writing.

🌀 References

Canavor, Natalie. 2016. *Business Writing Today: A Practical Guide.* 2nd ed. Thousand Oaks, CA: Sage.

Handley, Ann. 2014. *Everybody Writes: Your Go-To Guide for Creating Ridiculously Good Content.* Hoboken, NJ: Wiley.

Horton, Sarah, and Whitney Quesenbery. 2013. *A Web for Everyone.* Brooklyn, NY: Rosenfeld Media.

Kimble, Joseph. 2012. *Writing for Dollars, Writing to Please: The Case for Plain Language in Business, Government, and Law.* Durham, NC: Carolina Academic Press.

King, Stephen. 2000. *On Writing.* New York: Scribner.

Kupersmith, John. 2012. "Library Terms That Users Understand." *LAUC-B and Library Staff Research.* https://escholarship.org/uc/item/3qq499w7.

Plain English Campaign. 2016. "The A–Z of Alternative Words." Plain English Campaign: Fighting for Crystal-Clear Communication since 1979. Accessed May 25. http://plainenglish.co.uk/free-guides.html.

PlainLanguage.gov. 2015. "Federal Plain Language Guidelines." PlainLanguage.gov. Accessed May 20. www.plainlanguage.gov/howto/guidelines/FederalPLGuidelines/index.cfm.

Strunk Jr., William, and E. B. White. 1999. *The Elements of Style.* 4th ed. New York: Macmillan.

Zinsser, William. 2006. *On Writing Well: The Classic Guide to Writing Nonfiction.* 30th Anniversary ed. New York: Harper & Row.

Using Authentic and Active Voice

YOUR WRITING SHOULD BE GENUINE and believable. To best reach your readers, use conversational style, strong nouns, and active verbs. In this chapter, learn how an authentic and active voice makes your writing more accessible, understandable, and relatable to your readers.

Writing Like You Talk

Write Authentically

Librarians are service-oriented and want to please their customers. Being friendly and accessible in your writing helps you reach this goal. As you would in person, try to convey a friendly, helpful, honest voice in your writing.

For your content to sound natural, it's a good rule of thumb to write like you talk. If someone understands your message spoken out loud, they will probably understand your message written out. Zinsser writes:

> It's true that the spoken language is looser than the written language, [but] the growing acceptance of the split infinitive, or of the preposition at the end of a sentence, proves that formal syntax can't hold the fort forever against a speaker's more comfortable way of getting the same thing said—and it shouldn't. I think a sentence is a fine thing to put a preposition at the end of. (2006: 40)

Writing in this natural style will make you sound authentic—more like yourself. This helps you build trust with your readers, making them more willing to listen to what you have to say.

Think about your most complex, challenging content: terms of service, policies, procedures, and legalese. This type of content often sounds like a robot created it. But is it possible to take even the most challenging content and make it human and believable? Difficult, yes. But absolutely possible.

BUT I RAMBLE ON WHEN I TALK

A word of caution that you might not benefit from *literally* writing the way you speak. Perhaps you're a real talker, and in day-to-day conversations you use long, rambling sentences rather than complete sentences. Sometimes a spoken sentence will consist of multiple tangents and details, with few pauses or punctuation. Of course, you want to avoid this problem in your writing. As mentioned in chapter 4, you should keep sentences short. You can certainly set off content with parentheses or dashes, but as a general rule, try to have no more than one set of parentheses—or dashes—in a single sentence. Rather than writing exactly how you talk, make sure that when your content is read out loud, it sounds like a real person talking. It should sound like something you would be proud to say aloud in front of a room of people.

Use Words You Use in Real Life

Pay attention to your vocabulary. In real life, would you say, "Let us utilize our strategic partners to achieve shared vision?" Unless you are an administrator speaking to a room of other administrators, you probably would not. In everyday conversation, it's doubtful you would call people your "strategic partners," but you would call them your colleagues. You also might not use the term *shared vision*, but you may regularly talk about your goals. So you are more likely to say something like "Let's get together with our colleagues to better reach our goals." Notice this simple change in vocabulary gives the words a different personality, while keeping the essence of the message the same. The second example sounds more human and believable, and is more likely to resonate with your readers.

Each word carries meaning, and choosing the right words isn't always easy. But it's often easier than you think. In fact, Stephen King advises writers to *"use the first word that comes to your mind, if it is appropriate and colorful. If you hesitate and cogitate, you will come up with another word—of course you will, there's always another word—but it probably won't be as good as your first one, or as close to what you really mean"* (2000: 118). If a word made sense when you first wrote it on the page, try leaving it there. Don't spend precious minutes fussing through the thesaurus to ultimately find a word that sounds flashier but less authentic.

Don't misunderstand—the thesaurus is a great tool. So is the dictionary. They can provide you with inspiration as well as an expanded vocabulary. But if you, as the writer, have to look something up in a dictionary, it's probably not the best word to get your intended message across. You don't want your readers to have to pause to look something up. If you're stuck on a particular word, a better option than Merriam-Webster is to simply ask a colleague (or a potential reader), "Does this sentence make sense?" or, "Can you think of a word that would work a bit better?"

Jargon was covered in the last chapter, but it also comes into play as you attempt to write like you talk. In daily conversations with colleagues, you incorporate jargon: department acronyms, project team names, and library speak. But you wouldn't use the same terms when talking with library patrons. So when you aren't sure if something is jargon, ask yourself if it's a term you use in real life with your audience. If you are writing a webpage for a student audience, is it a term you would use when talking with an actual student at the reference desk? If you are writing slides for a presentation to your library board, are they words you would use when speaking with a board member over coffee? What level of explanation would you use in a conversation with an audience member, if jargon is unavoidable? The same level of explanation applies in your writing.

Read Out Loud

Since writing the way you speak makes content more understandable, it's good practice to read your content out loud. How does it sound? Can you imagine saying it directly to a member of your audience? Does it sound natural? First, read it out loud to yourself. Make edits, and then read it out loud to a colleague. Make more edits, and then take it to the streets.

Content guru Steph Hay recommends using the "Mom Test" to measure the quality of your writing. Is your content something you would read out loud to your mom? Do you sound like yourself? Would your mom understand what you're talking about? Think of someone in your life who knows you well and who you trust to give you candid feedback. You can actually pick up the phone and call this person. It could be your actual mom, a trusted relative, or a close friend. See what this person has to say about your content. If the person you pick is like many moms, she won't hesitate to point out your mistakes and encourage you to make improvements where needed (2012). If the Mom Test doesn't work for you, read your content out loud to an actual member of your audience. But pick someone who will be completely honest with you, like your mom would.

Write as a Conversation

In most cases, use conversational language to better connect with your readers. If you are creating a sign, imagine talking with your building visitors. If you are writing an article for your newsletter, imagine talking with your subscribers. If you write as if you are talking to them directly, they are more likely to feel a connection with you, and your message is more likely to resonate.

It's generally okay to use first and second person. It better connects your content with the intended audience by placing them within it. In most writing, address the readers as *you* and your organization as *us* or *we*. Say things like "You can help us improve the library" and "We are here to help." Beware of calling readers "customers," "patrons," or "clients." Speaking in third person sounds less authentic and puts a barrier between you and your audience.

On websites and other interactive mediums, it is especially important to treat your content as a conversation. Think of your web content as a conversation initiated by the

Table 5.1. Revisions to Reflect Human, Conversational Style

ORIGINAL SENTENCE	REVISED SENTENCE
Librarians are here to help.	We're here to help.
Customers are advised . . .	We advise you . . .
Dissertation Room applicants must be PhD candidates to apply.	You must be a PhD candidate to apply for a Dissertation Room.
For patron convenience, there are many locations to renew library cards.	Renew your library card at one of our many locations.
Library cards can be renewed . . .	You can renew your library card . . .
Group account permissions are now active in the departmental Box folders.	We have activated group account permissions in the departmental Box folders.
There are many strategies one can employ to minimize issues of cheating and plagiarism for online assessments, but there are times when instructors need solutions that help them monitor students' online work.	There are many ways to minimize cheating and plagiarism, but sometimes you need solutions that help you monitor students' online work.
The increased utilization of mobile devices for content consumption places demands on publishers to be more adept at engaging on mobile devices.	Almost everyone now uses mobile devices to access content, placing demands on publishers to make their content mobile-friendly.

site visitor (Redish, 2012). As the writer, it is your job to satisfy that conversation by answering visitors' questions and allowing them to reach their goals.

Adjusting your content to read like a conversation will make your writing more direct and digestible. Table 5.1 shows examples of how to rewrite sentences to reflect a conversational style, using first and second person and speaking directly to readers as if you were sitting across the table from them.

Relaxing and Having Fun with It

Loosen Up

The English language is incredibly complex, and you can find hundreds of books on proper syntax and composition. Some fundamental understanding of grammar is without a doubt important: follow a style guide if you have one, avoid typos, and make sure you don't have grammatical errors that confuse your meaning. Get an excellent editor, especially if you are writing for publication. But remember that what is considered correct usage and acceptable grammar is a moving target.

Zinsser writes, "Usage has no fixed boundaries. Language is a fabric that changes from one week to another" (2006: 38). This means that in much of your daily writing, there are few hard-and-fast rules. Because of the fluidity of rules in the English language, you can get away with being a bit risky in your writing. It's important to fix typos and significant errors, but you're not in a high school English class. If you do break a rule, the worst thing that can happen is you have to make an edit later. Focus on the clarity of your content, not the grammar.

Let go of presenting yourself as an über-professional. It's okay to be a bit casual in tone, since you are trying to convey information to your readers as if they were your friends, family members, or colleagues. Handley and Chapman encourage writers to "worry more about creating remarkable content; worry less about being professional" (2012: 38). Professionalism is a good thing, but when you try hard to appear professional, it's easy to fall into the trap of buzzwords and jargon. You become less believable and lose your readers before they reach the second paragraph. Of course, there are different levels of formality. For public-facing content, your defined voice should guide how casual you can be using specific guidelines, lists of terminology, and examples (see chapter 12).

Use Punctuation Wisely

Punctuation within and at the end of sentences helps establish the flow and flavor of your content. Use appropriate punctuation to break up your text and express your mood, but watch out for elements in your writing that make you appear stodgy or long-winded.

For example, the semicolon can make you sound old fashioned and serious. Zinsser went as far as to say, "There is a 19th-century mustiness that hangs over the semicolon" (2006: 72). Certainly the semicolon serves a purpose, but overuse can harm your voice and make you seem less human, so use it with discretion.

Dashes are usually more approachable than semicolons and parentheses. Take the sentence: "You can enter the building after 9 p.m.; just remember your library card" versus "You can enter the building after 9 p.m.—just remember your library card." Either is acceptable, but the second has a slightly different tone. When you are tempted to use a semicolon or put something in parentheses, try a dash and see what it looks like.

Parentheses are also a good tool for setting some content apart from the rest, but when used frequently they can make content seem disjointed and bureaucratic. They often force the reader to switch gears midsentence, or several times within a paragraph. Avoid writing multiple sentences or thoughts within a single set of parentheses, or using them as a way to add unnecessary, tangentially related content. Here are some examples of when using parentheses stiffens the tone and makes content harder to understand:

- For me, the key thing would be how it authenticates, and then how one could view results on the back end (for an entire class, for everyone taking the assessments, etc., so that one could understand where students have difficulties, etc.—whether or not one could build in remediation).
- Of course, if we say this, we actually have to do it (which means really pushing for faculty to be engaged and present, to always work with them on related assignments, etc.). I do not support us just saying yes to face-to-face instruction without looking for things in return (for the benefit of the students and also so that we can be more efficient and effective in our work).

Better examples of using parentheses that provide useful detail and actually improve the tone are as follows:

- If you'd like to check this out and give me feedback (on design and content), please do.
- Supplies (notebooks, pens) are available on the fifth floor.

While some punctuation marks can make your content appear formal, others can make you seem overly cheerful, silly, or excited. Take the exclamation point. It serves a useful purpose and can add fun and candor to your writing, but when overused—or used poorly—it can be problematic. You shouldn't use more than one exclamation point in a paragraph. And you certainly shouldn't have two sentences back-to-back ending in an exclamation point. A good use of an exclamation point might be, "Win $1,000 just for writing a research paper!" A poor use might be, "The library is open until midnight! Book a study room online!" Similarly, watch out for multiple exclamation points in a row, or even worse, the question mark–exclamation mark combination (!!???!!). This particular usage can freak out readers before they've even read the content. So unless that's what you're going for, it's best you avoid it.

Emoticons are punctuation for the digital age and are used frequently to express one's mood, especially in casual conversations over email and text. Like the exclamation point, these can be useful to indicate emotion, but annoying when overused or used inappropriately.

Use Contractions, Fragments, and Conjunctions

It's acceptable (and better) to regularly use contractions. It's usually better to say, "You don't have to register" rather than "You do not have to register" and "We won't share your information" rather than "We will not share your information." The use of contractions in the right spots helps you sound human. That said, you don't want to *only* use contractions or you might appear to be unprofessional and lose trust. There can be a fine line between a casual tone and an unprofessional one.

Complete sentences aren't always necessary, either, and fragments play a useful role. They can help with succinctness and make it easier for readers to scan through informational content. It's also okay to begin sentences with conjunctions, such as *and*, *but*, *so*, and *because*. In fact, while there is a widespread belief that this is grammatically incorrect, as many as 10 percent of sentences begin with conjunctions (Whitman, 2014). And nobody is complaining.

Maybe Use Slang and Colloquialisms

Consider how slang and colloquialisms fit into your overall voice. You probably want to steer clear of slang, such as *dude* and *LOLZ*, for the most part, unless your defined voice is exceptionally casual. But some colloquialisms could be okay in the right context. For example, it could be okay to call students "Wildcats" if that's your school's mascot, or say, "What's happening?" on the landing page of your human resources account system. Maybe even words such as *awesomeness*, and *epic fail* are appropriate in some contexts, such as social media. Just be sure to consider any nonnative speakers in your audience—you don't want them to be thoroughly confused by your word choice. Again, go back to your audience, your messaging, and your voice and tone to determine how casual or witty you should be (see chapters 2, 3, and 12).

Have Fun

If you're relaxed and comfortable letting go of the rules a little, you'll find writing naturally more enjoyable. It shouldn't be a stressful process. Writing is an incredible, human talent and can be a lot of fun. Your readers will notice if you care about the content and are having a good time writing it, and will be more likely to stick around. As Handley and Chapman explain, "Your point of view should have an element of fun. And what's more, you should be having fun doing it. If you aren't having fun creating content, you're doing it wrong" (2012: 38–39).

⑥ Using Active Voice

Active Voice Is Best

If you have studied the craft of writing, you've probably learned that active voice is the way to go. It's taught in practically every writing course and mentioned in every book on writing. It's the fourteenth rule in the *Elements of Style* (Strunk and White, 1999). Zinsser tells writers to "use active verbs unless there is no comfortable way to get around using a passive verb. The difference between an active-verb style and a passive-verb style—in clarity and vigor—is the difference between life and death for a writer" (2006: 67).

Active sentences are easier to read and understand. They are bolder. They help you cut to the chase and remove the fluff. Passive voice, on the other hand, makes your meaning vague and harder to follow.

Write in Active Voice

Active voice, at its core, means your sentences have a noun and an active verb. The subject of your sentence is doing something itself, rather than something passively being done to it. You can quickly identify a sentence that uses active voice once you identify the subject and the verb. For example:

- You can obtain additional information on our website. (*You* is the subject, and *obtain* is the verb.)
- The director told the curators that the exhibit would run through the summer. (*The director* is the subject, and *told* is the verb.)

The good news is active sentences are easy to write. They tend to be what people write (and what they say) naturally. If you find yourself floundering over a sentence that just doesn't feel right, step back and notice if you are falling into a weaker, passive voice.

USE PRESENT TENSE

It's easier to use active, direct voice when you are writing in present tense. Obviously, you can't write in present tense all the time since sometimes you'll be talking about the past or the future. But when in doubt—and when you have the option—favor present tense. Let the current goings-on drive the sentence. For instance, "We are compelled to close the building at midnight due to safety concerns" is better than "Safety concerns put us in the position of being compelled to close the building at midnight."

Avoid Passive Voice

When the subject of the sentence isn't actively doing anything, you have a passive sentence. Passive sentences make the writer appear timid and safe. To the reader, they sound boring and bureaucratic. Stephen King writes, "Two pages of the passive voice—just about any business document ever written, in other words, not to mention reams of bad fiction—make me want to scream. It's weak, it's circuitous, and it's frequently tortuous, as well" (2000: 123).

A clear indicator that you have a passive sentence is when the writer unnecessarily uses some form of the verb *to be*, such as *am, is, are, were, being,* or *been*. Earlier, you read two active sentences. Now notice the use of the verb in the same sentences rewritten in the passive voice:

- Additional information *can be* obtained on our website.
- Curators *were told* by the director that the exhibit would run through the summer.

Notice the tone of the sentences has changed now that the subjects aren't actively doing anything. It sounds dry and stuffy. Policy and procedure content tends to be filled with this type of passive language. You might see sentences similar to:

- The form is to be filled out by applicants in person at the office.
- Fines may be paid by patrons online.

You can easily reword these passive sentences to be active:

- Applicants should fill out the form at the office.
- Patrons can pay for fines online.

Or, bringing in conversational language, you can make these even better as:

- Fill out the form at the office.
- Pay for fines online.

In table 5.2, you'll find more examples of passive sentences revised to use active, as well as simpler, language.

USING PASSIVE VOICE TO BE DIPLOMATIC

Passive voice is occasionally appropriate. Because it allows you to not give credit for an action, it can be a tool for writing diplomatically when you're facing a heated issue. Don't use passive voice to skirt around issues when it's better to be direct, but do use it to spare feelings and approach serious conversations in a respectful way. It can help you avoid placing direct blame or passing judgment before you know all the facts. For instance, you might want to say, "All of the reports were submitted late," rather than, "All of you submitted your reports late." Knowing when to use passive voice to engage in respectful dialogue is a learned skill that can help improve your professional relationships.

Table 5.2. Revisions to Reflect Active Voice and Simpler Language

PASSIVE	ACTIVE
Eligibility will be verified.	We'll verify your eligibility.
Print cards can only be reloaded with the same value that is listed on the front of the ticket.	You can only reload print cards with the value listed on the front of the ticket.
A number of improvements have been made to the system in order to reduce the number of duplications in search results.	We made improvements to reduce the number of duplications in search results.
These statistics have been gathered from various sources, and therefore original source of data or date published may not be available.	We gathered these statistics from various sources, so original sources may not be available.
Software must be installed on a personal computer.	Install software on your personal computer.
After conducting interviews of faculty, students, and administrators, the collective knowledge gathered was used to develop requirements for an RFP.	We collected knowledge through interviews of faculty, students, and administrators to develop requirements for an RFP.

Picking Nouns and Verbs Wisely

Use Strong Nouns

While verbs indicate the action in sentence, nouns represent the things doing the action. In informal, conversational writing, the primary noun is often *you* or *I*, so you won't have to think much about it. But when you start writing about other things, you have lots of options.

It's best when the noun in your sentence is a person, place, or thing. This sounds obvious, but in a lot of difficult-to-read sentences, the noun can be hard to make out. A lot of times, especially in business and academic writing, people use what Zinsser calls "concept nouns" (2006: 75). They are abstract and intangible. Think of the main noun in this sentence: "The traditional culture of the organization leads to an inability to move forward quickly on technological initiatives." The primary noun—the one doing the action—is "the traditional culture of the organization." This is problematic because it is a concept rather than a thing. It's not really the *culture* that is causing the situation; it's the *people* within the culture. What the writer is really trying to say is, "Staff members are traditional, making it hard to move forward quickly on technological initiatives." By changing from a concept noun to a concrete noun, the sentence becomes much easier to understand. It also sounds more human. Other examples of concept nouns (which often include prepositions) are:

- The environment
- The context of the situation
- The collective thinking by the community
- The discussion
- The process in the department
- The recommendations to the committee

These terms certainly make sense in some contexts, but if you are tempted to use them as the primary noun in a sentence—as the thing doing the action—pause and reconsider. Is there a less abstract noun that could take its place if you reword the sentence slightly? Are there people involved who aren't mentioned in the sentence? If you are writing on a topic that involves people, be sure to mention people. If you are talking about a particular service, resource, or report, mention it. Strong nouns include:

- Staff members
- Students and faculty
- The committee
- Campus administrators
- The service
- The database
- The report

As you select nouns, remember to avoid jargon, buzzwords, and corporate speak. Maybe instead of "technological initiatives" you could say, "tech-focused projects." And instead of "anticipated professional development activity" you could say, "travel plans." Choose concise nouns that your readers understand and that best represent the message you're trying to get across.

Avoid Several Nouns in a Row

Passive phrases and sentences often involve several nouns in a row, which are difficult for readers to digest. You'll often see these as titles on webpages, subject lines on emails, and names of reports. Take for example:

- Instruction Consultation Request Form
- Submissions for Workforce Planning Requests File
- Associate Librarian Retention Review

You can write these same concepts more effectively by breaking apart the nouns and using active verbs:

- Request an Instruction Consultation
- Submit Your Requests to the Workforce Planning File
- Review the Associate Librarian for Retention

Paying attention to lengthy noun phrases and restructuring them like this increases understanding while reducing the cognitive load of your readers.

Use Strong Verbs

Select active, strong verbs. As mentioned in chapter 4, a well-selected verb can often make adverbs and adjectives unnecessary. A strong verb can also replace longer phrases that carry similar meaning. For example, "We *came upon* a photograph in the archive" could be replaced with "We *discovered* a photograph in the archive." The meaning stays the same, but the word *discovered* makes the sentence stronger.

Beware of the dull verbs *have*, *get*, and *made*, and try replacing them with stronger ones. For instance, instead of "let's *have* a meeting," just say, "Let's *meet*." And instead of "We are *going to get* new furniture for the conference room," try "We are *purchasing* new furniture for the conference room."

And avoid hiding the action in nouns instead of verbs by tacking on variations on the word *is*. So rather than writing "We *are* in support of," just write, "We *support*." Rather than "I *am* hesitant to," just write, "I *hesitate* to." And be careful of similar roundabout language that dilutes the verb. Replace "We will get started on" with "We will start," "She made the announcement" with "She announced," and "Make the decision" with "Decide." You get the idea.

Also, try replacing multiple verbs with one substantive verb. So instead of "Regularly *support and position* workers so they can *perform better* in the future," you could write, "Regularly *mentor* workers so they can *excel* in the future." Updating the verbs changed the meaning slightly, but kept the same intention while sharpening up the sentence.

Selecting strong, active verbs is especially important if you are using the verbs to direct readers to do something. If you are writing an email to webinar registrants, you might say, "To access this webinar, attendees must get the latest software." In this instance, you should use a stronger verb that is more reflective of what the attendees will need to do. A better, more active sentence is "To access this webinar, attendees must *download* the latest software." Even better is to address the attendees directly, treating the content as a conversation: "To access this webinar, download the latest software." The implied subject is the reader. The active verb is *download*.

◎ Key Points

Use authentic, active, conversational language. It's easier on the reader and will strengthen your content. Remember:

- Writing like you talk will help you sound human.
- It's not English class, so it's okay to break the rules a little.
- Active voice is best.
- Strong nouns and strong verbs make for the strongest sentences.

You've now considered the best approaches when it comes to style and word choice. In the next chapter, you'll dive into some particular components for structuring your writing: titles and headings.

◎ References

Handley, Ann, and C. C. Chapman. 2012. *Content Rules*. 2nd ed. Hoboken, NJ: John Wiley & Sons.

Hay, Steph. 2012. "Being Real Builds Trust." A List Apart. August 28. http://alistapart.com/article/being-real-builds-trust.

King, Stephen. 2000. *On Writing*. New York: Scribner.

Redish, Janice (Ginny). 2012. *Letting Go of the Words: Writing Web Content That Works*. San Francisco: Morgan Kaufmann.

Strunk Jr., William, and E. B. White. 1999. *The Elements of Style*. 4th ed. New York: Macmillan.

Whitman, Neal. 2014. "Grammar Girl: Can I Start a Sentence with a Conjunction?" May 29. www.quickanddirtytips.com/education/grammar/can-i-start-a-sentence-with-a-conjunction.

Zinsser, William. 2006. *On Writing Well: The Classic Guide to Writing Nonfiction*. New York: Harper & Row.

Writing Titles and Headings

QUALITY TITLES AND HEADINGS set the foundation for useful content. A title provides an entryway to your writing and can quickly engage or bore your reader. Headings form a content outline and can give it a logical, navigable structure. In this chapter, learn how useful titles and headings, along with the power of parallelism and consistency, strengthen your content and make it easier to follow.

Pick a Good Title

Titles Matter

Good titles are critical. They get your reader's attention (or don't). They can start you off on the right track or doom you for failure. They give readers a first impression, setting the stage and creating expectations for subsequent content. So make sure every title you write makes sense to your readers and does your content justice.

Most content you write has some kind of title. It's usually the first thing your readers see and it briefly describes the content that follows. Your title could be a:

- Document title (e.g., report, handout, manual)
- Webpage title

- Email subject line
- Blog post or news story headline
- Title slide of a presentation
- Article, book chapter, or book title
- Front page of a brochure
- Headline on a flyer, poster, or digital sign
- Name of an event or exhibit
- Name of a committee or taskforce

Whether or not you would call all of these examples "titles" or put them in title case, they serve the same purpose. The front page of a brochure has brief wording describing what's inside, such as "Information for Donors." Other print materials tend to have something similar describing the rest of the content, such as a flyer titled "Change in Hours" or a class handout titled "Advanced Searching Exercise." If you are naming an event, exhibit, committee, or taskforce, it will likely end up as a title in some form in the future—whether it's on a webpage, a news story, or a print program. In all cases, the qualities of a good title are the same: meaningful, succinct, and taking into account the reader's context.

TITLE CASE VERSUS SENTENCE CASE

What level of capitalization should you use in titles and headings? Title case means capitalizing the first letter of all significant words, as in "Information for Online Students." If using sentence case, you only capitalize the first letter of the first word, as in "Information for online students." Titles tend to be written in title case (hence the name, "title case"), but it's acceptable to use sentence case in some circumstances. Sentence case is more informal, approachable, and easier to read. It's customary to use sentence case for emails, signage, and on the web. If writing a more formal piece, such as a professional presentation, official report, or journal publication, title case is more appropriate.

If you are using sentence case for headings, use it for associated titles, too. Although headings are often sentence case even if titles are title case. Whatever you do, be consistent. All titles should be either title case or sentence case, and all headings should be either title case or sentence case.

Consider Your Readers' Context

Think about your audience and what likely brought them in front of your content. How did they find it? What is their frame of mind? What is important to them? Why should they care about what you have to say? In most cases, the title of your content will be the first thing they see and will be the deciding factor as to whether or not they continue reading. The title can also make a difference as to whether they find or notice your content in the first place.

If you expect readers to find your content through a search, use their search terms in your title. This is obviously relevant for web content, but is also relevant for documents in a shared storage space, emails, and any other case where content is stored in a searchable system, either now or in the future.

Consider your reader's frame of mind. If you know your readers are in a hurry, keep your title brief and make it crystal clear why they should care. If your readers are stressed out, perhaps your title can help ease their mind. If your readers are bored, perhaps your title can give them something to get interested in and excited about.

Especially if you are competing for your readers' attention, take into account what motivates them. What keeps them up at night? What would make their lives easier? They aren't required to care about what you have to say, so think about how your message will best resonate with them. Test your assumption that the content you're writing is, in fact, relevant to their lives. If it is, then see if you can come up with a title that assures them it's worth reading more.

Use Words Your Readers Use

Titles should be approachable and quick to understand. When possible, avoid jargon. In body content, you can describe any words your readers might not know, but titles need to be succinct, making it hard to both use jargon and explain it in the same breath.

A poor example of a title on an old library webpage is "Patron-Driven Acquisition (Also Known as On-Demand Information Delivery)." This is not one, but *two* specialized terms. The title includes both because the name of the service had recently changed, but it was still a new concept that most users outside the library world hadn't heard of. While "Patron-Driven Acquisition" and "On-Demand Information Delivery" are both adequate names for the service, interpreting their true meaning requires guessing on the part of the reader. A better title would be "Getting Books at Your Request." This title explains what the service *is* rather than what it's *called*. People are more likely to keep reading since the title speaks to them directly and tells them why they should care. Then, within the content of the webpage, the official title of the service can be used and explained.

This same rule applies to promotional materials. Imagine a brochure that has on the front page "Interlibrary Loan, Document Delivery, and Express Retrieval Services." As a visitor not familiar with these terms, would you be likely to pick it up? Now imagine if the front page was instead to say, "Get Books and Articles You Need, When You Need Them." The second version speaks to readers directly using plain language and lets them know why they might want to keep reading. This change in language makes the brochures more approachable and visitors are more likely to pause and take a chance at reading the rest of the content.

Make It Meaningful

Strive for clarity, specificity, and authenticity. Your title should reflect the content it represents. There should be no ambiguity and no surprises when the reader gets past the title to the crux of your content.

While you may want it to be enticing, don't write a catchy title that grabs readers' attention but doesn't live up to the hype. The last thing you want to do is disappoint your readers and lose their trust. So avoid exaggerations such as:

- Ace Your Assignments with Five Simple Research Steps
- How Our New Makerspace Is Changing Up the Rules Forever
- Take This Two-Minute Survey and Make a Better Library Future

These titles contain empty promises. Your research steps might be simple, but they alone can't promise students they'll ace an assignment. And your makerspace could be contributing to innovation, but it's hardly changing the rules *forever*. And maybe survey results could be used to make some strategic decisions, but gosh it's hard to make a survey that only takes two minutes, and is it really going to make that big of a difference to the future of the library?

Avoid hyperbole that makes you seem inauthentic. When hyperbole is used haphazardly, your readers will soon lose their trust in you as an organization or a professional. Better, more realistic, and still-compelling titles are:

- Five Simple Steps to Improve Your Research Assignments
- How Our New Makerspace Helps Reinvent What Libraries Can Do
- Take This Short Survey and Guide the Future of the Library

You also want to avoid ambiguous titles that tell the reader little if anything about the content within. For example, be careful about writing such vague email subject lines as:

- Update
- Meeting
- Recap
- Award
- Interesting Article

More meaningful titles save the time of the reader while setting up an expectation of the content. For example:

- Update on Strategic Planning
- Department Meeting Cancelled
- Recap of Web Designer Interviews
- ACRL/IS Innovation Award—Call for Nominations!
- Article on Service Design in Libraries

These titles have enough specificity to make them meaningful. This will help the readers not just at the time but also in the future if they need to locate historical information.

Reflect Any Call to Action

Are you asking the reader to *do* something? Too often, it is not clear from the title. If the goal is for the reader to proceed with some action, your title should include an active verb. Take, for example, these possible email subject lines or titles of forms:

- Scholarship Application
- Feedback Form
- ACRL/IS Mentoring Program

It isn't clear from these titles if what follows is just information or if the reader can actually do something. Better titles that reflect the role of the reader would be:

- Apply for a Scholarship
- Send Me Feedback
- Join the ACRL/IS Mentoring Program

By starting out with a verb rather than a noun, you make it clear to the reader that a response or course of action is both possible and expected.

Keep It Succinct

Succinctness is important in all writing, but especially with titles. A verbose title is immediately off-putting. When writing a title, include only essential elements. Every word and punctuation mark should serve a purpose.

As mentioned in chapter 5, it's bad practice to use too many nouns in a row. These cause cognitive overload and are difficult to understand on first pass. Sadly, titles are often culprits of the too-many-nouns-in-a-row syndrome. An example of a title suffering from this syndrome: "University of Arizona Libraries Travel and Professional Activities Review and Revision Taskforce Charge." This type of document is hard to title because it inherently includes a taskforce with a really long name. You probably can't avoid including it. Ideally you could come up with a more succinct name for the taskforce, such as "Taskforce on Professional Development," but if you're stuck with a longer name, try breaking up the nouns. And if it's an internal document, you probably don't need to spell out the full name of your library. The title becomes slightly more understandable as: "Charge for the Travel and Professional Activities Review and Revision Taskforce." But think of the possibilities if the taskforce had a more succinct name. You could then have a title as nice as, "Charge for the Taskforce on Professional Development." Are you more likely to read something with this concise name? Probably. It is more approachable and understandable.

You should be able to read a title aloud in one breath and remember it after reading it once. If you have to pause to breathe while reading it, if you can't repeat it aloud without reading it again, or if it takes up more than a single line in a document, it's probably too long. Try to keep your title to ten words or less, and use short words with fewer syllables. If you're struggling to keep it short, review some of the techniques from chapter 4. There is almost always another word you can omit.

Break Up the Title If Needed

Being succinct is often easier said than done, especially if you're working on content that has a lengthy official name. It can be hard to find the balance between meaningfulness and succinctness. Sometimes, breaking apart the title using a colon or subtitle is a good approach when you have no other options.

In the earlier webpage example revised to, "Getting Books at Your Request," you might get pushback from stakeholders that it's important to include the official name of the service in the title. This could be important to the users who learned the name of the service as well as important to promoting the service as part of a larger marketing plan. This is where you need to balance user goals and organizational goals. In this case, an alternative could be to include both. They could be combined into a longer title, broken apart with a colon, or broken into a title and subtitle:

- Getting Books at Your Request through On-Demand Information Delivery
- Getting Books at Your Request: On-Demand Information Delivery

- On-Demand Information Delivery (title) Getting Books at Your Request (subtitle)

Depending on the format, space, and technical limitations, any of these could be reasonable possibilities.

A more extreme example is a press release title such as, "Notices of Funding Opportunities: First Round of Funding for FY 2016 National Leadership Grants for Libraries and Laura Bush 21st Century Librarian Program." Boy, that's a doozy. But just being the content writer, you obviously can't change the official name of the grants, and it's important to mention the relevant year and that the funding opportunities are now available. You already tried to break it up somewhat by using a colon, but it still creates two full lines of text on your webpage. And it won't even fit in your email subject line. So what do you do? You can first merge some wording, "Notices of Funding Opportunity" and "First Round of Funding," into one message: "First Round of Funding Now Available." Then your best option might be to break it up into a title and subtitle. So something like:

- First Round of Funding Now Available (Title)
- National Leadership Grants for Libraries and Laura Bush 21st Century Library Program (Subtitle)

This is a bit better, but still a mouthful. Since this is actually trying to cover two different funding opportunities, you could take it further and see if it's possible to break them out. Perhaps the title of the announcement becomes, "First Round of Funding Now Available for FY 2016" and you create two headings within the body of the press release—one for the National Leadership Grants and one for the Laura Bush 21st Century Library Program. In addition to making the title easier to process, it has the advantage of adding structure to the content with headings.

Bring It All Together

In table 6.1, see examples of real titles and recommended revisions. The changes aim to make the content more meaningful, adding detail where needed to make it clear what content lies within and what is expected (if anything) of the reader. At the same time, the goal is to be succinct, where every word serves a purpose. If words ran together or caused confusion, they were broken apart into manageable chunks. Notice how much easier it is to process the titles in the right column.

Pick Good Headings

Headings Matter

Headings serve a number of purposes. Readers often skim through them to understand what the content is all about as well as to find specific pieces of information. In a digital form, they might navigate through them with a screen reader. Whatever the context, thoughtful headings help your readers:

- Get a sense of the overall content
- Identify what content is included

Table 6.1. Revisions to Make Titles More Meaningful, Succinct, and Action-Oriented

TYPE OF TITLE	ORIGINAL TITLE	REVISED TITLE
Email subject line	Annual Faculty Survey: Opportunities for University-Level Service via Participation in Shared Governance	Volunteer to Participate in Faculty Shared Governance
Document title	University of Arizona Libraries Travel and Professional Activities Review and Revision Taskforce Charge	Charge for the Taskforce on Professional Development
Online form	In-Depth Research Consultation Online Request Form	Request a Research Consultation
Press release	Now Available—Introducing Our New Spatial Data Discovery Portal	Explore Our New Spatial Data Portal
Blog post	Website Navigation Updates and Improvements Based on User Research Conducted	New Website Navigation Based on Your Input

- Understand how the content is organized
- Find the content most relevant to them

Not all content requires headings, but any content extending past a few paragraphs could benefit from them. And lengthy documentation, such as a handbook, is cumbersome without them. Can you imagine reading this book if its chapters didn't have section headings to break up the content? How often have you skimmed through a book like this one to get a sense of the content or find a particular piece of information?

The rules that apply to titles also apply to headings. When you craft your headings, make them relevant to your readers and use active, conversational voice when possible. Make them meaningful yet succinct, and pay attention to how they flow from one section to the next.

HEADINGS IMPROVE ACCESSIBILITY

In the digital world, headings have semantic meaning: they are for structuring content and giving it hierarchy. So make sure you use them for this purpose. Screen readers allow visually impaired users to identify headings, access a list of all the headings within content, or jump to content by heading. In documents and slides, headings can appear as a functional menu. This makes it much easier for users to navigate, so it's important to identify headings as actual headings and treat them as structural components to your content. In HTML, this means using the <h1> to <h6> tags. In Microsoft Word and Powerpoint, it means using the built-in heading styles.

Use Headings to Organize Your Content

Headings are a key component of structuring your content, so they work best when crafted with a logical order in mind. How you order them depends on how you expect people to access, read, and navigate the content.

A common practice is to place headings in order of importance, from most to least important. This mirrors the inverted pyramid style discussed in chapter 3. It works well for informational content, such as news stories and information about services. What do your readers want to know most often to least often? One example could be on a webpage about your equipment lending service. With a title of "Borrow Technology," you might then have headers:

- Laptop (most common)
- Tablet (somewhat common)
- Camera (less common)
- Voice Recorder (least common)

Another option is to order things chronologically—the same order in which they would take place in time. This works well for directions that reflect steps in a process or system, such as tutorials, research guides, how-to manuals, and training documents. In the case of a research guide, you could organize headers as:

- Select Your Research Topic
- Narrow Your Research Topic
- Search for Sources on Your Topic
- Incorporate Sources into a Research Assignment

This ordering is logical since you anticipate that researchers will select their topic, then narrow it, then search for sources, and finally incorporate those sources into their assignments.

Chronological—and at times reverse chronological—ordering also works well if you're dealing with things that have a clear association with time, such as case studies, historical data, news stories, or event listings. For instance, your headers could be, "Upcoming Exhibitions," then "Current Exhibitions," then "Past Exhibitions."

One last obvious option is to organize headings alphabetically. As with all options, this only makes sense if readers will approach your content this way. Only use A–Z ordering if you anticipate readers will be looking for their content alphabetically or there is simply no other logical way to order things (i.e., there is no priority order nor element of time). For instance, a list of journal titles, databases, library departments, or disciplines may work well in an alphabetical order. For example, you may order library departments in your directory as:

- Administration
- Circulation Department
- Research and Learning Department
- Special Collections

However you choose to order your headings, make sure it's putting the reader experience first, focusing on how readers are most likely to approach, navigate, and interact with your content.

Use Strong Verbs in Headings

As covered in chapter 5, using strong, active verbs is good practice in general. Headings are no exception. Using verbs in your headings contributes to conversational style and forms a stronger connection with your reader.

If your content leads readers to take some course of action, active verbs in the imperative work especially well. For example:

- Submit a Request
- Check the Status of a Request
- Cancel a Request

Active verbs are also appropriate for instructional and how-to content. Perhaps you have a training manual that would benefit from headings like:

- Register for an Account
- Confirm Your Email Address
- Customize Your Profile

In this book, many of the headings start with imperative verbs. Take a look at the first section in this chapter, titled "Pick a Good Title." In that section, the majority of headings start with active verbs in the imperative, including:

- Consider
- Use
- Make
- Reflect

Because this is a practical guide that teaches readers how to do something, it's a natural fit to use imperative verbs in the headings. But this practice is useful even when the reader isn't necessarily doing something as tangible. For example, "Learn How to Self-Publish" is a more intriguing title than the more passive "Self-Publishing Information." And "Share Your Research" speaks directly to the reader, as opposed to "Research-Sharing Opportunities." If you find yourself writing a noun as a heading, see if there is an opportunity to add a verb that would make it more active, direct, and compelling.

If imperative verbs don't seem appropriate for your content, gerunds (verbs ending in *-ing*) are a good alternative. They allow you to sound active without sounding bossy. For instance, if you have a "Friends of the Library" webpage, you may have headings such as:

- Donating to the Library
- Attending Fundraising Events
- Volunteering
- Getting in Touch

Gerunds aren't as direct as the imperative, but they get the same message across while avoiding coming off as pushy. They are still a better option than a more passive, noun-based heading, such as "Donations to the Library" and "Fundraising Events."

Use the Five *W*s and One *H* (Sometimes)

For informational content, a logical heading structure may revolve around your readers' most common questions: who, what, where, when, why, and how? This is especially true for content describing library services and events. For example, if you have a 3D printing service, appropriate headings on your website could be:

- About 3D Printing (what and why)
- Who Can Use It (who)
- How Much It Costs (how)
- How to Submit a Request (how, when, and where)

In this case, some of the headings actually include the words *who* and *how*. This works sometimes, but the questions are often reflected without them, especially in event or exhibit descriptions. For instance, a poster about an event may include such headings as:

- The Program (what and why)
- The Speakers (who)
- Location and Date (where and when)
- RSVP (how)

In both the above examples, it's unnecessary to use verbs. You could try to squeeze them in and end up with such headings as "Learn about the Program," "Meet the Speakers," and "Find Out the Location and Date." This isn't bad, and sounds more conversational, but it makes the headings longer and doesn't add significant meaning. Succinctness is key, so it's best to remove the unnecessary words.

Use Questions as Headings (Sometimes)

For some content, organizing by question works well. Again, it goes back to the readers' goals and context. If they have questions that need to be answered in a particular sequence, a conversational question-and-answer format could do the trick. This isn't unlike the Five *W*s and One *H* idea, but it's writing the headings out as actual questions.

If you are writing content about your room-booking service, for example, rather than having passive headings like "Reservation Policies" and "Locations," you can use headings like:

- What Rooms Are Available?
- Who Can Reserve One?
- For How Long?

Another good example might be on a page about a library award:

- How Do I Apply?
- What Are the Rules?
- How Are Applications Evaluated?
- When Am I Notified If I'm a Winner?

These headings work well because they are succinct, easy to understand, and follow a logical order based on the primary needs of the audience.

Be cautious when using questions as headings, though, as they are easy to do poorly. If you are putting together a webpage about visiting your reading room, for example, you might be tempted to structure headings such as:

- What Do I Have to Bring to the Reading Room with Me When I Visit?
- Do I Need Money for the Lockers?
- What Are Your Policies Related to Food in the Reading Room?
- Am I Allowed to Bring My Laptop into the Reading Room?

These quickly become verbose and unwieldy, and don't sound like the sort of questions visitors would actually ask. Rather than using questions in this case, a better option might be:

- What to Bring
- What Not to Bring

There are debates among user-experience experts about whether frequently asked questions are good practice. Generally speaking, like many things, they can be done well and they can be done poorly. So try to avoid these common problems:

- Writing too many questions
- Using too many words in your questions
- Putting the questions in no particular order
- Basing the questions on the organization's assumptions, not the readers' actual needs
- Using question-and-answer format all the time, even when it isn't appropriate

Bring It All Together

Writing and ordering headings to best meet the needs of your readers takes practice and patience. And there is a careful balance in capturing meaning and conversational style while also being succinct. Take a look at the examples in table 6.2, where headings are revised to be more useful and understandable. Imagine how these headings could both help readers understand the breadth of content in front of them as well as guide them to information they need.

ⓖ Be Consistent

Use the Power of Parallelism

There is a simple technique that can make an incredible impact on the quality of your writing: parallel construction. This technique aligns your messaging and makes your content easier for readers to process. Parallelism is important across all your content, but is essential when it comes to content readers are likely to skim in a sequence, such as titles, headings, and lists.

Table 6.2. Revisions to More Useful Headings

TITLE OF CONTENT	ORIGINAL HEADINGS	REVISED HEADINGS
Information for Students	• Study Rooms and Spaces • Technology Lending Service • Research Assignment Assistance • Writing Assistance	• Find a Place to Study • Get the Technology You Need • Do Better on Your Assignments • Sharpen Your Writing Skills
Write and Cite	• Citation Management Tools • Citation Guide • Guide to Avoiding Plagiarism	• Organize Your Sources • Cite Your Sources • Avoid Plagiarism
Computer Lab	• Computer Access • Locations of Computers • Printing Service	• Who Can Use the Computers? • Where Are the Computers? • How Can I Print?

Make Your Titles Consistent

Readers will often skim through several related titles in a row, whether they are browsing menus on your website or looking through documents in a folder. Imagine you have a drop-down menu on your website that includes the titles:

- Improve Your Research Skills
- Finding Sources in Your Discipline
- Grant Funding Searching

These titles are fine in some respects (they are concise and include useful verbs), but they don't follow the same grammatical structure. They jump from the imperative verb *improve* to the gerund *finding*. And then they end with three nouns in a row: "Grant Funding Searching." The reader's brain has to switch perspectives twice to process what's being said. Take a look at this revision, where each title now begins with a gerund:

- Improving your research skills
- Finding sources in your discipline
- Searching for Grant Funding

With one small change, this list became much easier to process on first try. Yet it's still not quite right. There is inconsistent use of title case and sentence case. Title case is used in "Searching for Grant Funding," (since the first letters in *Grant* and *Funding* are both capitalized), but sentence case is used in the other two titles (where only the first letter of the first word is capitalized). These titles also might benefit from a stronger, imperative verb rather than a gerund. A final revision that embraces directness, consistency, and parallelism is:

- Improve Your Research Skills
- Find Sources in Your Discipline
- Search for Grant Funding

Make Your Headings Consistent

Headings are often read in sequence—even more so than titles—and especially by readers skimming through to find what they need. So your headings ought to align in tense, style, and structure. Imagine skimming these headings on a webpage:

- Study Room Application
- Learn about Our Collaborative Learning Space
- Reserving the Library Instruction Room

Again, these headings aren't terrible—they reflect meaning—but they could be better. The first one is a noun, the second uses an imperative verb, and the third uses a gerund. Much better, structurally consistent headings (that reflect the same content) are:

- Apply for a Study Room
- Learn about Our Collaborative Learning Space
- Reserve the Library Instruction Room

When reading the revised headings, your brain doesn't have to switch tenses or perspectives. Meaning is clearer and reading or skimming is less onerous.

Make Items in Lists Consistent

Lists are another place where parallelism (or lack of it) has big impact. Readers often skim lists of content, whether a list of bullets or a numbered list. Especially in lengthier lists, parallelism goes a long way to saving the time of the reader.

Imagine you are visiting a website for the first time to learn more about a tool for measuring library data and impact. You are considering purchasing it for your team. Following the heading "Why Choose Our Product?" you see this list:

- It is really easy to setup.
- It is fully integrated with analytics.
- Magical Retroactive Analysis
- Set up an account and get access to reports.
- Find Key Business Insights in a Few Clicks.
- Helpful insights will be found in our reports
- Your analytics reports are complete
- Data you can trust
- Save time, energy, and make yourself look like a hero by using our reports.

This tool might be just what your team needs, but this list is fraught with problems. There are some complete sentences ("It is really easy to set up"), some fragments ("Data you can trust"), and some standalone nouns ("Retroactive Analysis"). Punctuation is inconsistent, with some sentences ending in periods and some not. Sentence case is used some of the time and title case other times, and it's not clear whether it's intentional or a mistake. Some pieces speak directly to the reader ("Set up an account"), while others use passive voice ("Helpful insights will be found"). And there is no particular order to the list. It is almost as if different people wrote each bullet point. As the reader, you very well may have lost trust in the product at this point. At minimum, you are probably confused about what the product actually does and are frustrated in the lack of clarity this list provides.

Try reading this alternate list. Again, imagine it follows the header "Why Choose Our Product?"

- Easy account setup
- Full integration with analytics
- Retroactive analysis
- Complete, insightful reports
- Trustworthy data

By combining redundant messages, improving consistency, reordering, and applying parallelism, this list just became a whole lot easier to understand.

So when writing lists of content, make sure you are thoughtful and consistent. This goes for bulleted lists and numbered lists as well as series of content following a colon. If one instance is a complete sentence, they should all be complete sentences. If one is a fragment, they should all be fragments. They should all be written in the same tense, from the same perspective. When you read them out loud, there should be a seamless, logical flow from one to the next.

If you find yourself stumbling over a relatively short list of content, check for a lack of parallelism. It is likely the culprit. More on effective use of lists will be covered in chapter 7.

Embrace Consistency

Aim for consistency within sentences, across paragraphs, and across the breadth of your content to improve reader understanding and experience. If you are using present tense, stick with it. Verb tenses should not change unless you are intentionally transitioning to another perspective. Similarly, voice should stay consistent across all your content, and tone should only change for a deliberate purpose. If you are writing in a conversational style using *we* and *you*, keep it going. Avoid switching your style or perspective midstream. It confuses readers and breaks flow.

Even within individual sentences, pay attention to parallel construction. Avoid the common grammatical problem of "false series." These occur when you break the flow by switching perspectives in the midst of a list of things. For example, don't say, "I will join the committee, the taskforce, and update my service documentation." You are *joining* the committee and *joining* the taskforce, but then you switch to *updating* the documentation. Alternatively, you can say, "I will join the committee and the taskforce then update my service documentation." If a list of things in a sentence doesn't sound quite right, check if you have a false series.

Consistency with word usage is also important. If you are writing a tutorial on using the library catalog, you might want to use *journal* or *periodical*, but don't use them interchangeably unless it's absolutely clear what you're referring to. Readers can get confused if you refer to things differently when you are talking about the same thing.

Consistency in your writing will improve your reputation as someone who is reliable, understandable, and direct. Pay attention to consistency from the highest level down to the smallest details. Answer the questions:

Table 6.3. Revisions to Improve Consistency

TYPE OF CONTENT	ORIGINAL	REVISED
Titles	• Research by Subject • Course Guides • Tutorials and guides • Sharing your research	• Research by Subject • Research by Course • Improve Your Research Skills • Share Your Research
Headings	• Writing Literature Reviews • Copyright Guide • Write and Cite	• Write a Literature Review • Learn about Copyright • Write and Cite
List	• Click here to search for Books and Media. • CD and DVDs • Finding theses and dissertations • Journals and Magazines	• Books and media • CDs and DVDs • Theses and dissertations • Journals and magazines
Sentences	You should contact the archivist. Patrons can call her anytime.	You should contact the archivist. Call her anytime.
Sentence	Fill out the online survey, the print form, and email your supervisor.	Fill out the online survey and the print form, and then email your supervisor.

- Do you use title case or sentence case in titles? What about headings?
- Do items in your list include punctuation or not?
- Are items in your list fragments or complete thoughts?
- Do you use ampersands (&) or spell out *and*?
- Do you use first and second person?
- Are you writing in present, past, or future tense?

See table 6.3 for more examples of improving consistency within titles, headings, lists, and sentences.

⊚ Key Points

Thoughtful titles and headers, along with consistency at all levels, strengthen your content. People are more likely to read and understand it on the first try. Remember:

- Your title provides your readers with the first impression of your content, so make it count.
- Headings are key to organizing your content and making it accessible.
- Parallelism is a great tool for improving your content's readability and approachability.
- Consistency is key.

Titles and headings lay the foundation for clarity in meaning and structure, but what about the core of the content? In the next chapter, you'll learn the fundamentals of using lists and tables appropriately, simplifying the complex by formatting body content in the most usable way.

Using Lists and Tables

ONE OF THE BIGGEST COMPLAINTS you'll hear from readers is, "It's too much text! I don't want to read that!" It's true that walls of words can be intimidating, especially if you are in a hurry and don't have time to read something word-for-word. In addition to keeping it simple and reducing the length of your sentences and paragraphs, take advantage of tools that break apart your content and make it more approachable: bulleted lists, numbered lists, and tables. In this chapter, you'll learn when to use each tool and for what purpose, and common pitfalls to avoid.

Bulleted Lists

Use Bullets to Create White Space and Allow Skimming

When readers complain about "walls of words," they often make the obvious suggestion: use bullets to break apart the content. So if your content seems long, consider using bullets. This is one of the things bullets do best: they create white space and make content more approachable.

Lists are easy to skim and scan, so they work especially well when you expect readers to browse through your content. Perhaps they want an overall sense of the content or they are looking for a particular item of interest. Bullets are excellent tools for writing:

- Features of a service, tool, or resource
- Policies
- Lists of examples (like this one)

Use Bullets for Series

If you have a series of more than two items you want to communicate, bullets might be a good way to present them. This is especially true on a webpage where skimming is expected. Rather than writing a long sentence with a list of everything, as in "All of our libraries have computers, printers, scanners, and technology help," write the items out in bullets, as in "All of our libraries have:

- Computers
- Printers
- Scanners
- Technology help

If you find yourself using the word *including*, *such as*, or *for example* in a sentence, followed by a series of items, you probably have a candidate for a bulleted list. Other series of related content could include:

- Qualifications in a job posting
- Duties in a job description
- Types of materials in a collection
- Project updates
- Changes to a service or resource

Use Bullets for Lists of Options

If you are presenting a number of options or alternatives, a bulleted list is your best bet. Readers can easily get a sense of how many options there are and find a specific item they might be interested in (Redish, 2012). A list is much more approachable than several long, compound sentences. For example, you might use bullets to list out:

- Library locations
- Types of databases
- Collection areas or specialties
- Software options
- Ways to contact the library

Keep Bulleted Items Short

Items in bulleted lists should generally be individual sentences or sentence fragments. Using two shorter sentences is acceptable, but once you get to three sentences you are no longer making the bullet useful. Don't make paragraphs with bullets. This defeats the purpose of the bullets—you may as well just indent the paragraph. If bullets make your content more readable than paragraphs, even when the content is the same, you may need to change your formatting. Adjusting line height and space between paragraphs and headings, as well as breaking things up with useful headings, can make content more readable and is more appropriate than trying to use bullets to achieve the same result. (See chapter 13 for more on formatting.)

Use Consistency in Bullets

Remember the power of parallelism discussed in chapter 6, and make sure items in bullets are parallel. Start each item with the same element of speech and avoid mixing full sentences with fragments.

Perhaps you want to communicate about how your team has improved an advanced search feature within a tool you maintain. You might list out the product improvements, such as:

- Added a tool tip to identify the icon upon hover
- Search data is now maintained due to an enhancement
- Improvements to the list of content types in advanced search

This content can be edited slightly to make it parallel:

- Added a tool tip to identify the icon upon hover
- Made an enhancement so that search data is now maintained
- Improved the list of content types displayed in advanced search

Notice that the second iteration is much easier to read quickly and comprehend, though the meaning remains the same.

Bullets can be short sentences or fragments and can use title case, sentence case, or lowercase. Whatever you decide, be consistent. If there is punctuation at the end of one bullet, make sure there is punctuation for the rest, as well.

Avoid Repetition in Bullets

Try to avoid starting bullets with the same words. This repetition is unnecessary and can make content harder to read. For example, if you are writing about visiting your reading room, you could write:

- Remember to bring change for the lockers.
- Remember to bring a sweater (it gets cold in the reading room).
- Remember to be quiet (other people are studying).

These all start with "Remember to." To simplify, you could simply introduce the bullets with "Remember to" followed by:

- Bring change for the lockers.
- Bring a sweater (it gets cold in the reading room).
- Be quiet (other people are studying).

⬳ Numbered Lists

Use Numbers for Instructions and Steps in a Process

Numbers imply a sequence of things—most often, a set of instructions or list of steps. If a reader's goal is to find out how to do something, they may skim your content to look for a numbered list, anticipating that this is how instructions will be presented. Using numbered lists (rather than bullets) makes it clear to readers you are writing things out in a particular order. It allows them to quickly see how many steps there are and locate their place within the sequence. It also makes it more likely they will complete all of the steps correctly and in order (Redish, 2012).

If you write out instructions in sentence form, you can end up with complex paragraphs of content and the dreaded wall of words. Even a basic example that teaches readers how to browse films in foreign languages can be complex: "First go to the catalog. Then type * in the 'Any Field' search box. Select 'Video/Film' in the 'Format' drop-down menu. Finally, select the language in the 'Language' drop-down menu, and then click 'Search.'" Notice how much easier it becomes to follow this when written out as steps in a process:

1. Type * in the "Any Field" search box.
2. Select "Video/Film" in the "Format" drop-down menu.
3. Select the language in the "Language" drop-down menu.
4. Click "Search."

If your readers are asking a "How do I . . . ?" question, you should probably use a numbered list to explain the answer (assuming it takes more than one step). If you find yourself using transitions such as *then* or *next* several times, you also probably have something that would work as a numbered list. The list also gives you the advantage of not having to use repetitive transition words, since the numbers take care of transitioning for you. You will have a much easier time writing instructions using numbered lists, and readers will have a much easier time following your instructions.

Use Numbers to Indicate Order

Another good use of numbered lists is to present things in a sequential order. Perhaps you want to indicate in what order the main outcomes of a project will happen, as in:

1. Creation of a project plan
2. Validation of the plan with stakeholders
3. Implementation of the plan
4. Evaluation of the plan

The numbers imply an order to the events. This use of numbers works well for outlining dependent tasks, steps toward a goal, or a progression of activities.

Use Numbers to Indicate Priority

You can also use numbers to indicate level of priority or importance. This is most common in such cases as "top ten" lists. Library examples might be your top three reasons for visiting the library, top five study tips, or top ten books recommended by library staff. These work well independently, but can cause confusion if you place them near other numbered lists. So be cautious when using numbers for different purposes within the same piece of content.

Don't Use Numbers Arbitrarily

Writers often use numbered lists when they'd be better off using bulleted lists. If you use numbers, readers may interpret the list on first glance to be a list of steps in a process or list of things in some sort of order. If the list of things has no particular, intentional order, a bulleted list is the best option.

For example, if you are listing things you can do with a new tool, you might write:

1. Manage references and citations
2. Annotate articles
3. Add and organize papers
4. Share and collaborate with peers

On first glance, this can be interpreted as a list of actions you would take in order. In reality, users of the tool could do any or all of these things in whatever order they like. Writing these out in bullets makes this more apparent:

- Manage references and citations
- Annotate articles
- Add and organize papers
- Share and collaborate with peers

USING ROMAN NUMERALS AND *A, B, C*

Variations on the numbered list are the Roman Numerical list (I, II, III, IV) and the Alphabetical List (A, B, C). These are often used to create an outline of content, and are useful options if your readers would benefit from the structure these provide. For example, in a lengthy document you can point to "section B" or "item VIII" more easily than "the eighteenth bullet."

Be thoughtful as you use these, though. While they don't imply steps in a process or priority order as directly as numbered lists do, they can imply an order of importance. For instance, if writing a job description and listing duties as A, B, and C, the candidates might assume that the most important duty is A, the second is B, and the third is C.

⑥ Tables

Use Tables for Numerical Data

The most obvious content to put in a table is numerical data (see table 7.1). If you are presenting service costs, a budget, or staff salaries, a table is going to be the best way to display the content. It helps you compare numbers at a glance.

Table 7.1. Example of a Table for Comparing Numbers

	OPERATING BUDGET	EVENT BUDGET
User Experience Department	$3,560	$450
Research and Learning Department	$2,000	$780
Access Services Department	$2,500	$800

Use Tables to Indicate Relationships

Tables are also great tools for presenting non-numerical data that has a relationship. In their basic form, tables are essentially a set of "if, then" sentences. The title of the first column can be read as the "if," and subsequent columns as the "then(s)" (Redish, 2012). Tables can help users understand trends and relationships between content and find quicker answers to their questions. It's often much easier to understand a table of content than the same content written in pure text format.

If you find yourself writing several sentences using similar language, you might have a candidate for a table. For example, "Undergraduates can check out seventy-five books for three weeks at a time. Graduate students can check out two hundred books for three months at a time. Faculty members can check out 250 books for six months at a time." This content is better presented as a table, as in table 7.2.

Table 7.2. Example of a Table for Related Content

	NUMBER OF BOOKS YOU CAN BORROW	HOW LONG YOU CAN BORROW THEM FOR
Undergraduate students	75	three weeks
Graduate students	200	three months
Faculty members	250	six months

If the answer to a reader's question is "It depends," you also may have a candidate for a table (Redish, 2012). For example, questions such as "What are your hours?" and "How much does printing cost?" may both share the answer "Well, it depends," because it depends on the library branch or the type of printing service. Examples of "it depends" and other related content appropriate for tables include:

- Library borrowing privileges by type of user
- Library branches and their associated hours
- Printing services and their associated fees
- Librarians and their phone numbers, office numbers, and specialties

Use Clear Column and Row Titles

Tables should have column titles, row titles, or both. These give structure to the table and make it clear what content is being presented. As you come up with appropriate titles, put the readers' questions at the forefront of your mind. What question(s) do your readers have that the table can help answer? What language would they use? In table 7.1, the column titles are "Operating Budget" and "Events Budget." The row titles are "User Experience," "Research and Learning," and "Access Services." These were labeled as such in anticipation of readers asking such questions as, "What is the operating budget for the Access Services Department?" and "What is the events budget for the User Experience Department?" This assumes the readers are familiar with these types of budgets and the names of these departments.

In table 7.2, the row titles indicate the type of library user, and the column titles indicate the borrowing privileges. These were also labeled with the readers' questions in mind, anticipating such questions as, "How many books can a faculty member borrow?" and "How long can undergraduates borrow books for?"

⊚ Key Points

When used well, lists and tables are great tools for bringing structure and clarity to your writing. Remember:

- Use bullets to present items, series, and options.
- Use numbered lists to present instructions, sequences, or priorities.
- Use tables to present related content.

You now have a set of tools to use across all types of content for improved clarity and structure. In the next chapter, you'll learn how to best write a particular type of content: information and instructions.

⊚ References

Redish, Janice. 2012. *Letting Go of the Words: Writing Web Content That Works.* San Francisco: Morgan Kaufmann.

WebAIM. 2013. "Creating Accessible Tables." WebAIM. October 25. http://webaim.org/techniques/tables.

Writing Information and Instructions

PERHAPS A MAJORITY OF THE CONTENT you write is information and instructions. For your external customers, it could be a sign in your building, policies on a webpage, or a how-to worksheet. Within your working environment, it could be a report, an email update, or a training document. Information and instructions aren't always the most exciting things to write or to read. But in this chapter, you will find out how even the beefiest and most boring content—such as policies—can become more readable, understandable, and perhaps even a bit of fun.

Writing Brochures and Flyers

Librarians often use print collateral to promote services and events. You tend to find racks of brochures in library lobbies along with flyers posted on walls, windows, and bulletin boards. These print pieces can be an effective way to educate and inform visitors, but require some thought to implement effectively.

Focus on Your Message

As discussed in chapter 3, you need to define your primary messages, and those messages should be front and center. If your readers only get through the first few lines (which is a definite possibility), they should have an understanding of your main point. Try to keep brochures to just a few main messages, and flyers or posters to just one single message. Don't allow your important messages to get lost in a sea of content.

As discussed in chapter 6, use a title that is meaningful to the reader. When your visitors are walking by, there is a good chance that the title is the only thing they will see. The title will help them determine whether the content is relevant or useful. If you have a brochure about your new print-on-demand book maker, try giving it an action phrase title, such as "Self-Publish a Book" or "Print a Book in Minutes." This speaks more directly to the readers' motivations than a passive, more ambiguous title of "Espresso Book Machine."

You are especially limited in space, so removing unnecessary content is a requirement. Review chapter 4 and see what words, sentences, or paragraphs can be removed without losing meaning.

Make It Fun

Brochures in a rack and flyers on a bulletin board are unique in that they depend on the reader stopping in their tracks to pay attention. Understanding your readers' motivations will ensure your content does what it sets out to do. Especially if your goal is to motivate readers to take some course of action (e.g., attend an event, try a new library service), experiment with making the content fun and exciting.

For example, if you have an author lecture series coming up, try coming up with a title that will get the attention of passersby. The title "Explore the Unknown Universe with Local Authors" is more likely to grab attention than "Local Science Fiction Authors Lecture Series."

Avoid Common Pitfalls

It's easy to create verbose brochures and flyers because you want to have robust content and make sure you answer all your readers' questions. It's easy to title something the name of a library service because that is what you know it as. It's easy to use passive voice to try and sound more academic and less direct. But all of these are common pitfalls of brochures and flyers that make them harder for visitors to read. To avoid these pitfalls:

- Have a meaningful, user-centered title.
- Stick to your primary messages.
- Use action phrases for headings.
- Avoid passive voice.
- Avoid putting too many nouns in a row.
- Keep sentences and paragraphs super short.
- Make content engaging and fun.

⊚ Writing Signage

Libraries, especially those that have large, multi-story buildings, tend to have a significant number of signs, some printed and some digital. Directional signs assist visitors in navigating the building. Promotional signs aim to raise awareness of a library service, event, or initiative. Other signs inform visitors of something relevant, such as the name of a service desk, policies, or instructions on how to do something. All of these signs play an important role in the experience of the building visitor.

Unfortunately, libraries have a tradition of creating signage that is inconsistent, confusing, and negative. Great progress has been made in recent years as more libraries are paying attention to the user experience, but there are still instances of poor signage in most library buildings (Stempler and Polger, 2013).

Focus on the Purpose

The first step to creating a useful sign is identifying its purpose. Think about both your visitors' and your organizational goals. What do building visitors want to do? What do they need to know? What do you want them to know about? Perhaps visitors need to be able to navigate through the stacks, so you create directional signs that identify call number ranges and names of collections. Visitors also need to know how to find specific books, so you create signs that provide instructions on how to read call numbers. Maybe your library has a new book-scanning service, so you also create promotional signs that explain how the new service can save people time and effort.

Whatever the purpose, keep your content focused. Remember, you have your readers' attention for only a short amount of time. Make it count.

Avoid Negative Language

As with most educational institutions, library buildings are places where you're not allowed to do certain things. While most libraries strive to be welcoming environments, they need to balance that with the need to keep their collections and technology intact, as well as to keep their spaces conducive to study and reflection.

It's quite likely that your library has at least a sign or two that tells visitors what they are not supposed to do: "No food or drink" and "Don't reshelve books" are common examples. Some less common, almost absurd examples include, "Do not chew on the headphone cords" and "No balloons" (Brandon, 2013). Often, these types of signs include all caps, red font, underlines, and/or exclamation points. While these policies exist for good reason, there are better ways to communicate. Using negative language can be patronizing and hurt your relationship with your visitors. As Leah White rightfully points out, "Such negative signage insults our patrons instead of guiding them or communicating policies in a positive and efficient manner" (2010: 23). You would rarely go to a commercial business and be bombarded with the negative or passive aggressive signage you may find in a library. To make your policy-driven signage more approachable:

- Write like you talk, not like a terms of service agreement.
- Say "please" or "thank you" (but usually not both) if you are telling visitors things they're not allowed to do.
- Don't use all caps, red font, underlining, or exclamation points.
- Explain (concisely) why the policy is in place.
- Give your visitors an alternative option (if there is one).
- When possible, tell your visitors what they *can* do, not what they *can't* do.

Some examples of revised signage can be found in table 8.1.

Table 8.1. Signs Revised to Be Less Negative

ORIGINAL SIGN	REVISED SIGN
ATTENTION: *No food or drink* in computer lab. Thank you.	Please enjoy food or drink on the first floor only. Help us keep the computer lab clean.
Quiet area! No talking.	This is a quiet area. Please keep talking to a whisper.
Cell phones are PROHIBITED.	Please silence your phones. You can take calls in the library lobby.
PLEASE do not reshelve books.	Leave books on cart for us to track and shelve.

Similarly, you might have signs that let visitors know a service or tool is currently unavailable. Perhaps your checkout machines are broken or your computer lab is full. Rather than writing institutional-looking "Out of order" or "Filled to capacity" signs, see if you can't bring a friendly, human voice to it.

For example, when the restaurant chain Chipotle ran out of an ingredient, they had a sign that said: "Sorry, no carnitas. Due to supply constraints, we are currently unable to serve our pork. Trust us, we're just as disappointed as you, and as soon as we get it back we'll let the world know." The most important message gets top billing, but it doesn't stop there. This sign explains the situation, is sympathetic, and lets the customer know what to expect. Similarly, Chipotle has a sign they place on their soda machines when they are out of order that states, "This soda machine is out of order. All that it currently delivers is heartache and pain, and possibly wet shoes." As these examples demonstrate, Chipotle consistently uses a lighthearted, fun, personable voice in their signage.

There are lessons to be learned from signs in the commercial world. Pay attention to signs you see when you visit a business, especially those ones you find especially helpful or interesting. When your study rooms are filled to capacity, perhaps your sign should say more than, "No rooms available." It could say, "Sorry, no rooms available right now. We wish we had more. Feel free to put your name on the waiting list and relax in our lobby in the meantime."

Format for Readability

Paying attention to readability is especially important with signage, as you are dealing with readers in a unique context: on the move. They can view signs from different angles and distances, and often have minimal time to take in any content being presented.

One rule of thumb is to left align any paragraph text on your signs. Never justify signage text. The even spacing between words and consistent alignment improves readability and quickens comprehension. This same rule exists for other content, and will be discussed in more detail in chapter 13, but centering text is especially prominent and problematic on signage. This habit should be removed from common practice.

One advantage of the signage format is you can use different sized fonts and get creative with spacing and graphical elements. Be sure to use a large font for the primary message(s) on your sign. Secondary messages can be typed in a smaller font. Use numbered and bulleted lists appropriately, as explained in chapter 7. Signs are especially prone to skimming by passersby, so take full advantage of tools that create white space and make content easier to scan.

Place Signs Thoughtfully

The placement of signs is incredibly important. Directional signs ought to be at the stop points where visitors need to make a decision on where to go next. Other informational signs ought to be placed at the relevant point of need for the visitor. Promotional signs ought to be at the places visitors might stop and pay attention. All signs need to be placed somewhere they are readable from a reasonable distance where you'd expect visitors to be located.

Avoid bombarding visitors with too many signs. The same way that website visitors get "ad blindness" on websites with too many advertisements, building visitors can get signage blindness when there is too much of it. Place signs strategically so that visitors will notice them.

And test the placement of your signs. Observe visitors navigating your building and see how well the signage is (or isn't) working. Use usability testing methods to test how well signs assist visitors in wayfinding throughout your physical space.

Avoid Common Pitfalls

Signs can be challenging to create. Even with the best of intentions, librarians can create signs that talk down to users, lack clarity, and are ripe with passive voice. To avoid these common pitfalls:

- Treat signs as a conversation with your visitors (use *you* and *we*).
- Place signs at the appropriate place in the building.
- Be direct, focused, succinct, and unambiguous.
- Pay attention to your voice and tone, and avoid sounding paternalistic.

⊚ Writing Policies, Terms, and Conditions

Consider the Reader

Policies can be the most challenging to write with the user in mind. Usually, little thought is given to how a user will interpret library policies. It's common to hear a librarian say, "Well, our patrons probably won't read this, but at least we can point to it if something goes wrong." While it is good to have something in place for when something goes wrong, this a pretty silly approach to content. If you are putting something up on your website or posting something on your wall, it should be something you expect and hope that your users will read. If you keep the policies succinct and well organized, there is a good chance users will at least skim them and get the gist of what you are trying to say. And it can serve the library's interests by actually avoiding the problem of "something going wrong" down the road.

To write policies well, you need to consider the expectations and motivations of your readers. Write with their interests in mind, not your own.

How often have you accepted terms and conditions on a website without reading them? Even though these terms often affect users' privacy and intellectual property rights, the sad fact is that few people take the time to read them before clicking the "accept" button. It's not surprising, given their complexity. Researchers who analyzed terms of service agreements from different websites found they average a reading level of a college sophomore and can take hours to read, or *years* if you are to read all of the terms for every website you visit (Fiesler and Bruckman, 2014). So clearly, these terms are not written with the intention that users will actually read them. They are written to satisfy the legal requirements. So if you want someone to read or understand something, don't put it only in a terms of service agreement. Even if they are well written, people have gotten in the habit of ignoring them completely.

Prioritize

In poorly written policy documentation, there tends to be a mishmash of content in no particular order. Included alongside each other are often:

- Information people really should know—the most important stuff
- Warnings about bad things that people probably won't do, but it's part of the policy and needs to be included anyway
- Details people don't care about right now, but might care about at some point later on
- Other details people don't really care about, and never will

For example, imagine you are writing policies related to your 3D printing service. There are a lot of details, and you need to figure out how to structure them. What are people going to really care about? When it comes to services, people usually care about:

- Time
- Money
- Outcomes
- Expectations

So people are going to want to know that 3D print jobs cost money, and how much. They want to know that it will take a day or two to process. They also want to know what to expect: that they will get an email when their job is complete and ready for pickup.

People care less about things like legal requirements, copyright specifications, and fiddly details. This doesn't mean this content isn't important or shouldn't be included, just that it should be less of a priority and placed under the more relevant, important content. Readers care less (or not at all) about:

- Legalese that doesn't affect them in any real way (e.g., "3D printers may only be used for lawful purposes")

- Warnings about things they would never do (e.g., "No one is permitted to create dangerous or obscene material")
- Things not relevant to them at this point (e.g., "Items not picked up in thirty days are recycled")

So as you structure your policies and agreements, put what readers want and need to know first. Everything else is secondary.

Use Second Person and Active Voice

One of the most infuriating things about policy documentation and terms and conditions statements is their overuse of third person and the passive voice. All too often, the reader is referred to in third person as something like the *patron, candidate,* or *registrant.* Sometimes, there is such prominent use of the passive voice that there is no clear indication of who does what, making the content even more difficult to follow. For example, take this statement:

> Complete service terms and conditions will be provided following application. Program participation may be terminated at any time. Enrollees have thirty days from the date enrolled to receive a full refund. After thirty days, enrollees will be reimbursed the pro rata share of any amount paid for any portion of the program period subject to cancellation.

What a doozy. As a reader, each sentence is hard to follow and the paragraph as a whole is exhausting to read. But by simply switching the point of view and speaking directly to the reader, notice how much more readable it becomes:

> After you apply, we'll send you our complete service terms and conditions. We may terminate your participation in the program at any time. You have thirty days from the date you enroll to receive a full refund. After thirty days, you will be reimbursed the pro rata share of any amount paid for any portion of the program period subject to cancellation.

Simplify and Write Like a Human

Try reading policy statements and terms of agreements out loud. Even in the above revision, there are still notable problems. The last sentence remains overly complicated: "You will be reimbursed the pro rata share of any amount paid for any portion of the program period subject to cancellation." This sentence sounds more like a robot is saying it than a human. The main message this sentence is trying to get across is that enrollees will receive a pro-rated reimbursement if they cancel after thirty days. A much simpler way to express this would be, "If you cancel after thirty days, you will receive a pro-rated reimbursement."

Legal information is especially hard to write like a human, but it can be done with a bit of time and effort. For example, you may ask users to check a box confirming they have read a copyright statement at the bottom of your interlibrary loan form. It may read as:

> The individual requesting materials via this electronic interlibrary loan form agrees to follow copyright law of the United States of America and to only use requested materials for individual, private study, scholarship, or research, or in accordance with federal fair use guidelines as available for electronic viewing. The individual must understand that requested materials used for teaching and instruction must be restricted to currently

enrolled students within the relevant course web page authenticated as such through mechanisms such as the course management system authentication system or other password-protected websites.

Removing unnecessary words, writing in plain language, and switching to first person make this cumbersome statement much easier to understand:

I agree to follow U.S. copyright law and to only use the requested materials for private study, scholarship, or research, or in accordance with fair use guidelines. I understand that materials used for instruction must be restricted to currently enrolled students (e.g., password-protected course website).

Avoid Common Pitfalls

Policies and terms are complicated and hard to write. But there are things you can do to make this type of content more approachable:

- Focus on your users' challenges and motivations, not your own.
- Put the most important, essential messages first.
- Use numbered lists and bullets to improve readers' ability to scan.
- Avoid library jargon, legalese, and policy-speak.
- Write like you talk and replace passive voice with active, direct voice.

◎ Writing Instructions

When Instructions Are Not Needed

Educating users is important, but too often instructions are written when they aren't needed. For example, instructions are often placed at the beginning of a form or survey, saying things such as "Fill out the form below" or "Fill in the required fields on this form." This instruction is unnecessary. The best forms and surveys require minimal, if any, instructions to fill them out. Users are familiar with forms and assume they need to fill out the fields, and indicating on the form fields themselves about what is required should be sufficient (more on writing forms in chapter 9).

Similarly, you shouldn't need a webpage with instructions on how to find something or do something on your website. If you do, there is probably something wrong with your website. Understandable, usable navigation should make many instructions irrelevant. For example, imagine you have a service called Express Documents that allows users to request scans of book chapters and articles. Website visitors interested in making a request find your webpage about Express Documents and it reads:

1. On the library main page, click on "Document Delivery" under the "Services" menu.
2. On the next page, click on "Log On to the Express Documents Request Form."
3. On the following page, enter your authentication number and click on the "Log On" button.
4. Next, fill out the request form with the required fields and click "Submit."

This example is the epitome of unnecessary instructions. At this point, users have already reached the page about Express Documents on the website. They don't need or want instructions on how to get to the request form; they just want to get to the request form. A better user experience would not list out instructions, but would just link the user directly to the form with an action phrase such as "Request a document scan." What the user does next is at the point of need—they follow an intuitive navigation path, fill out a form, and click a submit button. The last thing you want to do is ask your user to have a set of instructions in one hand while they are trying to navigate your website.

In Steve Krug's groundbreaking yet commonsensical book on web usability, he agrees that instructions are a common source of unnecessary words. He goes so far as to state, "Instructions must die" (2014: 51). So rather than cluttering up your webpages with instructions—which users are unlikely to read anyway—try to tackle the root cause of the issue: an unintuitive interface, navigation, labels, or content. In other words, make your website as easy to use as possible whereby users can quickly find information and complete relevant tasks. In most cases, instructions shouldn't be necessary.

When Instructions Are Needed

All that said, instructions obviously have an appropriate time and place. If you need to teach your users or colleagues something, you will provide them with instructions.

If you work in a public library, you likely host skills-based classes. You might teach patrons about computer privacy, job searching and resume building, and genealogical research. These classes may involve related web resources, handouts, and slide decks, all of which contain instructional content created for your students' one-time or ongoing use.

In an academic library, you might deliver information literacy instruction. This instruction may require you to create webpages, worksheets, and tutorials filled with how-to content. Perhaps you are teaching students how to read call numbers, find a streaming film, or recall a book that is checked out. Or you might be teaching them more critical conceptual skills, such as how to narrow a research topic, analyze results in a database, or incorporate sources into a research paper.

Back in the office, you may find yourself giving instructions to employees as part of their training. You might create a training manual, handout, or online lesson. Perhaps you are teaching them how to set up email rules in Outlook, find relevant documentation, or fill out a timesheet. Or maybe you are teaching them something more complicated like how to conduct a reference interview, manage volunteers, or conduct performance reviews.

Needless to say, instructions have their right time and place. You will have to write them, and your readers will benefit if you write them well.

Use Numbered Lists

In chapter 7, you learned that numbered lists are great for presenting step-by-step instructions. You also learned the power of parallelism. As you write instructions in a numbered list, use a parallel grammatical structure by starting each item with an imperative verb that speaks directly to the reader. For example:

1. Place the book on the scanner bed.
2. Turn on the machine.
3. Press the "Scan" button.

If you have more complex instructions where some steps include sub-steps or other details, you can expand to a multi-level list. For example, instructions on appointing somebody to a committee could read as:

1. Send an email call for faculty volunteers.
2. Give people one week to respond to the email.
    a. Aim for at least two volunteers.
    b. If you receive no volunteers and it's the last day, recruit individuals to volunteer.
    c. If needed, extend the call for up to three days.
3. From the list of volunteers, appoint a faculty member to the committee.
    a. Base your appointment on the established criteria.
    b. If you still have no volunteers and the deadline passes, you may appoint a faculty member who didn't volunteer.
4. Notify any volunteers who were not appointed.
5. Notify the volunteer who was appointed.
6. Notify all faculty members of the appointment.

If your instructions require more than two levels of structure, consider using headings or other structural elements to break things apart rather than trying to put everything in just one numbered list.

Use Structure and Headings

Instructional content is often more complicated than a list of steps and requires more structure. Many libraries create interactive tutorials that allow for robust, interactive content spanning multiple topics and learning outcomes. You also might create a content-rich guide broken apart into multiple sections, pages, or chapters. This entire book is a practical guide, and so could be considered a complex set of instructions.

Whatever you're dealing with, be sure to organize your instructions in a way that makes sense to the end user. Consider if users will want to skip from one section to the next or if they need to follow the content in order as written, because this can influence what you call things and how you organize. If you have a list of chapters or other form of navigation, use titles and headings that are meaningful, as discussed in chapter 6. If working in an online environment, make sure buttons and links are obviously clickable, and the words on navigation elements resonate with whoever is reading them.

Use headings to break apart more complex instructions, preferably action phrases that begin with imperatives and gerunds (Redish, 2014). Make sure headings use parallel grammatical structure. Avoid using lengthy questions (e.g., "Is it possible to renew a book after it was already past due?") or numerous redundant headings that begin with the same words (e.g., "How do I . . . ?" "How to . . ."). Write more effective headings by using action phrases, using parallelism, and omitting needless words, as demonstrated in table 8.2.

Be Clear and Consistent

Use unambiguous verbs. If your instructions are asking users to do something online, you will likely be repeatedly using the verbs *click* or *select*. Be sure to use just one of these options for consistency's sake and so the user won't wonder if they mean different things. If you decide to indicate certain elements with quotations, bold, or italics, do this consis-

Table 8.2. Revised Headings for Instructions

ORIGINAL HEADINGS	REVISED HEADINGS
How to renew a book How to pay a late fee	Renew a book Pay a late fee
How do I narrow a topic to something more manageable? How do I search most effectively?	Narrowing your topic Searching effectively
Tips as you start your search Using subject terms effectively Getting the full text of the article Citations	Start your search Use subject terms Get the article Cite the article

tently throughout the set of instructions. If you end a step with or without punctuation, do the same for the rest of the steps. If you have similar instructions elsewhere, be sure there is consistency across instructions, too.

Avoid Common Pitfalls

Educational content provides a public good and makes for better citizens, students, and employees. But it is easy to do poorly. To avoid creating ineffective instructions:

- Keep content consistent, parallel, and organized.
- Write in the readers' language and explain any jargon.
- Focus on your core purpose and remove any unnecessary content.
- Test content out with readers to make sure it works as intended.

Writing Memos and Reports

Formal memos and reports are often victims of bureaucratic and passive language. Even when writing for an internal library audience, take care to write in a way that is approachable. Assume that all your readers—including employees—are pressed for time and need to quickly absorb the information.

In a report on open access initiatives, for instance, you might find a sentence like "The Libraries provide programmatic education and advocacy related to open access and publishing to the campus through events, online tools and materials, and, where appropriate, by working with faculty and instructors to embed appropriate learning objectives into curricula or programs." This sentence is dry, complex, and hard to digest. Rather than a long compound sentence, the message can be conveyed in bullet points. The same general message can be written as:

We provide open access and publishing information to campus through:

- Events
- Online tools and content
- Working with instructors on their curriculum (where appropriate)

Reports and memos tend to be boring, and it can be tempting to get careless with your writing in this context. But you will be more successful if you follow the same practices you would when writing to an external audience. When writing such a document, be sure to:

- Focus on your core messages and remove anything unnecessary.
- Use a meaningful, parallel heading structure to break apart content and allow for skimming.
- Choose active voice over passive voice.
- Use bulleted or numbered lists and tables to break apart and present content in a more digestible way.

Key Points

Strive to create user-centered information and crystal clear instructions. Remember:

- Write brochures and flyers that are fun and easy to skim.
- Be purposeful in writing and placement of library signage.
- Write everything with the reader in mind, even policies.
- Only write instructions when they are necessary.
- Keep information and instructions organized, concise, consistent, and unambiguous.

Informational content is most of what librarians push out to readers. It tends to be one-way: you write the content, and the user reads the content. In the next chapter, it's time to move on to another type of writing, one that involves interaction with the reader: forms.

References

Brandon, John. 2013. "9 Very Specific Rules from Real Libraries." *Mental Floss*, February 10. http://mentalfloss.com/article/48843/9-very-specific-rules-real-libraries.

Fiesler, Casey, and Amy Bruckman. 2014. "Copyright Terms in Online Creative Communities." *CHI'14 Extended Abstracts on Human Factors in Computing Systems*, pp. 2551–56. ACM Digital Library. http://dl.acm.org/citation.cfm?doid=2559206.2581294.

Krug, Steve. 2014. *Don't Make Me Think, Revisited: A Common Sense Approach to Web Usability.* New York: Pearson Education.

Redish, Janice. 2012. *Letting Go of the Words: Writing Web Content That Works.* San Francisco: Morgan Kaufmann.

Stempler, Amy, and Mark Polger. 2013. "Do You See the Signs? Evaluating Language, Branding, and Design in a Library Signage Audit." *Public Services Quarterly* 9, no. 2: 121–35. doi:10.1080/15228959.2013.785881.

White, Leah. 2010. "Better None Than Bad: When It Comes to Signage, Nix the Negative." *American Libraries*, August 12. https://americanlibrariesmagazine.org/2010/07/12/signage-better-none-than-bad.

CHAPTER 9

Writing Forms

IN THIS CHAPTER

▷ How to structure forms with the reader in mind

▷ How to write unambiguous questions and field labels

▷ How to make forms more intuitive and approachable

SOMETIMES YOU WRITE TO GATHER information from readers, and a common way to do this is through forms. You prompt readers with fill-in-the blank questions along with options for them to select, perhaps using check boxes, radio buttons, or drop-downs. On the web, forms are prolific and necessary for many of the most meaningful tasks and interactions. Forms are notoriously annoying and nobody likes filling them out, so writing in this context has particular challenges. In this chapter, you'll learn how to make forms easier for readers to understand and less stressful for them to complete.

◉ Establishing Goals and Purpose

Define Your Users and Their Goals

Because forms serve a function, they often stand between users and their goals. Yet they are often cumbersome—fraught with complicated instructions, help text, and unnecessary fields. Luke Wroblewski (2008) argues that one of the biggest problems with forms is they are designed from the "inside out" rather than the "outside in." In other words, people create forms because the organization needs (or wants) to gather information from their customers. But by turning it around and looking at user goals and expectations, your entire approach may change.

So, as with other content, start by thinking about the people on the other end. Put your organization's need aside for a moment. Who are the people who are actually filling out your form, and why? What is the context that landed them on the form in the first place?

Most of the forms library users fill out are functional in nature—they get users closer to completing particular tasks. Library users depend on forms for crucial interactions, such as:

- Signing up for library cards
- Requesting or ordering materials
- Registering for a service
- Paying late fees
- Contacting the library

Since such forms are necessary to meet their goals, users might be willing to spend a little more time on them (up to a point). You have other forms that are less critical to users' goals, and their patience for lengthy forms is much less, such as:

- Providing feedback on a service
- Registering for events
- Making donations
- Subscribing to newsletters

Jarrett and Gaffney (2008) describe the following types of form users: readers, rushers, and refusers. It's possible that you're dealing with "readers" who will take the time to read associated content and instructions prior to filling out the form. This is often the case when the stakes are high, such as funding requests, performance evaluations, and perhaps the crucial interactions listed earlier. It's more likely, though, that your users are "rushers" who want to quickly complete the transaction and won't spend time reading nearby content. This is often the case for feedback forms and membership renewals. Sadly, you may have some "refusers" among your audience. These are users who get easily frustrated with forms and actually refuse to fill them out—it is not worth their effort. This means any reward they might get for completing the form does not make up for the time and energy it would take to complete it.

Identifying your users, their goals, and their frame of mind will allow you to build the most effective forms. It will help you:

- Avoid jargon or ambiguity
- Remove anything that isn't relevant
- Ask the right questions at the right time

By designing forms with users in mind, you will get more accurate responses and higher completion rates.

Define Your Goals and Scope

Defining your own goals in creating the form is another important step. It will keep you focused and encourage you to only include what's necessary. You want users to fill out your form accurately. When building a functional, task-driven form, think about what information is pertinent to the task. Try filling in the blanks: "We need to know _____ in order to _____." The second part of this statement is your goal. For example:

- We need to know the complete title and author(s) of the book in order to retrieve the correct book for the student.
- We need to know the size of the poster in order to print the correct size and charge the correct fee.
- We need the donor's address in order to send him or her a thank-you letter.

If you are writing a survey, you can use the same technique to clarify your goals and purpose. Everything within the survey should get you closer to your goals. Perhaps you have a goal to:

- Better understand why people use your website
- Find out about librarians' professional development activities
- Gather feedback on your strategic plan

Every question puts more work on your users and can reduce completion rates, so be wary of adding questions that don't serve a specific purpose. You want results that provide valuable, actionable data. Every question should matter.

Having clearly articulated goals for both those filling out the form and those analyzing its results sets a foundation for effective form content and structure. So try outlining such goals before starting work on a form—it will save you time and keep you focused.

ⓖ Keeping It Simple

No one *enjoys* filling out forms, so your main goal in creating a form is to make it as quick and painless as possible (Wroblewski, 2008). You can do this by removing anything unnecessary, keeping the content simple and on point.

Avoid Introductions and Instructions

Users generally skim over introductory statements (especially lengthy ones) and go straight to filling out the form. But this is okay, because when done well, most forms require little or no introduction. The title of the form should make its purpose obvious. The words describing the input fields should make it clear what the respondent is supposed to do.

Avoid beginning a form with unnecessary, obvious instructions such as:

- Fill out this form as completely as possible. Thank you.
- Please provide your information using the form below, and then click "Submit."
- To participate, please complete the following questionnaire.
- Use this form to [repeat title of the form].

Also avoid including instructions that talk down to users. These types of directions seem to assume your readers have never filled out a form before:

- Fill out all fields correctly.
- Fill out this form completely and accurately.
- Please print legibly.

- When you are ready to go to the next page, click the "Next" button.
- Once you have completed all of the information, press "Submit" to submit your application.

If instructions are necessary, see if it's possible to put them within the form itself—at the point of need. If you have information that people really should know before filling out the form, consider having it on its own page to give it prominence. This method is often used in research studies, where privacy or legal information is listed on its own page before users agree to start the survey.

Avoid Redundancies and Remove the Unnecessary

Forms are prone to including redundant content. You'll often find introductory text that replicates the title of the form. Perhaps you have a form titled "Email a Librarian" that then asks, "Would you like to email a librarian?" Similarly, you might have a form called "Request an Article" that starts out with "Use this form to request an article." Pay attention to such redundancies and remove them. As explained above, the title of the form is often all you need.

You can also try to simplify wording on your labels and questions, using the same techniques discussed in chapter 4. See table 9.1 for examples of simplifying labels and questions without losing meaning.

Table 9.1. Simplified Field Labels

ORIGINAL LABEL	REVISED LABEL
Email address	Email
Street address	Address
Which of our library locations do you visit most often? Select one of the following options.	Which of these libraries do you visit most often?
Where is your favorite place in the library? Why is it your favorite place? Please explain.	Where is your favorite place in the library and why?

Keep It Relevant

It is remarkable how many forms include questions or fields that aren't really needed. Wroblewski insists that you should put every question you are asking people to the test, since "people need to parse every question you ask them, formulate their response to that question, and then enter their response into the space you have provided. The best way to speed up that process is not to ask the question at all" (2008: 22).

Forms that have been around for a while often contain legacy questions that are no longer applicable. Don't irritate new library users by asking for their fax number or mailing address in order for them to sign up. If these fields are no longer necessary (or never were), it's time to remove them.

You can also hide content that isn't relevant to some users. On the web, conditional logic in forms can help with this. For instance, let's say you have a form for users to request digital copies of articles. Librarians want to know when articles are being requested by instructors for use in their courses. The form could have a field that asks, "Is this for a course you are teaching?" followed by other questions: "If so, what is the course?" "Have you taught the course before?" and "Would you like to discuss your course with a librarian?" For those users who are not requesting articles for a course, these subsequent questions are irrelevant. So you should use conditional logic so that the subsequent questions are only exposed if a user answer "yes" to the initial question.

Similarly, you might have content that only a segment of your audience is interested in. Perhaps your interlibrary loan form includes an "additional details" section that only advanced users would fill out (fields such as "DOI" and "ISBN"). To avoid displaying irrelevant fields to the rest of your users, you can collapse that section of the form, only expanding it for those who deem it relevant for them.

HOW SHORT SHOULD A FORM BE?

As with most content, succinctness should be a goal. But there is no magic number of fields or questions. It depends heavily on the users' goals and motivations. For users, the benefits of completing the form need to outweigh the effort they are putting into it.

⑥ Making It Easy

Be Consistent

Ensure that you are consistent in content, formatting, and voice. If you use colons after a field label, use colons after all field labels. If you use asterisks to indicate required fields, use them consistently in placement and styling throughout the form. If your field labels are justified left on the first page, make sure they are justified left on subsequent pages. If you use sentence case in one field label, use sentence case in all field labels. Don't switch between active and passive voice, or casual and formal tone. Consistency will allow users to digest the content more easily. They'll be less likely to make mistakes or get frustrated.

ALIGN FIELDS TO ALLOW FOR SCANNING

Use clean and consistent alignment to best allow readers to scan through a form and see what's expected. Use consistent layout across your forms and provide clear scan lines. Try to align field labels so that you can look over them without moving your eyes back and forth across the page.

Use Conventions

Forms are prolific, so there are many form conventions that your readers will be familiar with. There are common patterns used across the web especially.

One convention is how to indicate which fields are required and which fields are optional. People tend to assume an asterisk means "required," so marking required fields with an asterisk is your best bet. Be sure to include a legend that indicates what the asterisk means, and don't confuse users by using an asterisk to mean something other than "required" (such as "for staff use only").

When you ask a reader to select from a set of options, you have a choice between check boxes or radio buttons. Use check boxes if users can select more than one option and radio buttons if they need to select just one option. This is a standard convention and allows you to avoid unnecessary instructions as "Check all that apply" or "Select just one of the options below."

If you need an address, break it apart into fields: street address, city, state, and zip code (in that order). Don't ask readers to put their address in one large text entry field, or muddle up their thinking by asking for zip code before city and state.

If you need readers to select a date within a web form, use a calendar. This is much easier for users than asking users to select the month, then day, then year within drop-downs. It also makes it harder for them to input the wrong date.

Start paying attention to forms as you fill them out in your daily life. Conventions continue to evolve—especially on the web and on handheld devices—so it's important to keep up with the latest practices and changing user expectations.

Avoid Ambiguity

Watch out for ambiguity in field labels. On an article request form, don't just say "Title" but specify, "Article title" or "Journal title." On an award application form, rather than a vague label of "Status," try asking, "How are you affiliated with the university?" Ambiguity not only is bothersome to the user who notices it, but also can bias or even invalidate your responses. Ensure that your questions mean the same exact thing from one reader to the next.

Make It Accessible

Make sure that people using keyboard navigation (rather than a mouse) as well as people using screen readers can use your web forms. Users should be able to navigate from one input field to the next with a keyboard. Field labels need to be semantically marked up as field labels and should help text clearly associated with particular fields. Don't rely solely on physical relationship to other elements on the webpage—for screen readers, semantic meaning is essential.

Pay attention to the design of your input fields. In print, make sure they are long enough for a person with reasonable type size to fill in without going outside the field or having to squish letters together. This is especially true with email addresses that can be thirty or more characters long.

Provide Help Text

While some instructions aren't necessary, some are helpful, especially in more complicated forms with uncommon fields. *Microcopy* refers to snippets of relevant information. On forms, microcopy is often used as help text underneath or within input fields. Use help text for things like:

- Character requirements for a password (e.g., "five or more characters")
- Formatting requirements for a phone number (e.g., "520-555-5555")
- Advice on how to fill out the information (e.g., "Find your passcode on the bottom right of your library card.")
- Explanation of why the question is being asked (e.g., "This data is required by the university.")
- Examples of appropriate responses (e.g., "Examples: geography, medicine, history")

At the same time, don't clutter your forms with unnecessary help text. You shouldn't need to provide an example email address, for instance, because email addresses are prolific. Write help text only when it provides users with relevant information that will help them fill out the form accurately.

Be Inclusive

Be careful you aren't excluding anyone who might be filling out your form. If you are asking people to select a gender identity, don't limit them to "male" or "female"—include a "no response" option. If you are doing a campus survey and include a department drop-down, make sure you include every possibility. If it's impossible to include every possibility, have an "Other" or "Not applicable" option, and put it last in the drop-down. Respondents will feel excluded if their identity is not represented, and may leave a survey if they feel they are not part of the audience or can't answer a question accurately.

MOVING AWAY FROM CAPTCHA

For security reasons, web forms sometimes include a CAPTCHA: a colorful image with letters in it that you have to decipher and reproduce. The purpose is to ensure the person filling out the form is an actual human, not a robot. But many times, actual humans can't understand the thing and have to go through several attempts before getting it right. Fortunately, the days of CAPTCHA are nearing an end. Newer technology, such as Drupal's Honeypot module, will make CAPTCHA a thing of the past. So when possible, use a technology that keeps your forms secure but doesn't aggravate your users.

Make Error Messages Useful

In a web form, if someone fills out a field incorrectly or fails to fill out a required field, make the corresponding error messages clear. Users shouldn't be faced with puzzling or incomplete messages, leading them to troubleshoot the errors themselves.

If you are asking users to create a password and you have password requirements, make sure your error message makes it clear why the password is not valid. Don't simply write, "Your entry does not comply with the password policy." Rather, explain the details: "Your password must be at least eight characters long and contain at least one number."

Make the Next Steps Clear

In print, make it clear where the individual is supposed to mail or turn in the form (e.g. "When finished, place this form in the comment box at the information desk."). On the web, pay attention to the "Submit" button at the end of the form. Rather than labeling it simply "Submit," try giving it a specific, meaningful title that reflects the action. For example:

- Place your order
- Activate your account
- RSVP now

Once the respondent turns in the print form or submits the web form, he or she should know what to expect next. On a print form, this information could be at the end of the form or at the point at which they turn it in. On the web, this information should be on the confirmation page after the submission. However the information is presented, make it clear to the respondents:

- What you will do with their form information
- When (and if) they should expect a response
- What they should do if they have questions or concerns

For example, on a form people use to suggest new books for the library, the confirmation message could say: "We will carefully consider your request and email you our decision within two days. If you have questions in the meantime, call us at 555-5555."

⊚ Keeping It Organized

Create Sections with Headings

On longer forms, break content into purposeful sections and sequence those sections in a logical way. If organizing a form into sections, use meaningful headings. For example, your first heading could say, "Tell us about yourself," and the second, "Tell us about your request." The same way that headings allow readers to scan (as covered in chapter 6), headings in forms allow readers to know what to expect. This will also allow users to make sure they have all the required information up front before starting to fill out the form.

Put Related Content Together

As you think about sequence, remember that users expect certain fields to come first or last, and certain fields to be near each other. For example, the following fields are usually found in proximity, in this order:

- First name
- Last name
- Email address

Users will tend to expect personal information to be grouped together either at the beginning or end of the form. They'll also expect questions related to the particular service or topic to be together. If you have terms and conditions, they'll expect it to come last, and usually in the form of a box they are required to select.

Form structure varies and it all depends on context, but you should be able to identify some natural groupings. And if you have a complex, multi-page survey, your questions may build on previous questions. However you decide to structure your forms, be thoughtful in how you sequence content so that it has a logical, intuitive flow.

Consider Multiple Pages

While most forms fit nicely on a single page, others have an unavoidable level of complexity. In print, the number of pages matters less because users have access to all the pages at once. But on the web, having multiple pages means hiding content on subsequent pages. Sometimes this is appropriate, and sometimes it's not.

To make this decision, consider how your users will approach the form. Do they need to see the information in one place because there is a relationship between questions, and they might find value in viewing previous (or upcoming) questions? Is it important for readers to know up front exactly what information is expected? In that case, one long webpage could be better than a multi-page form. On the other hand, if there are three distinct sections or a sequence of distinct steps, and users won't need to see information from differing sections, splitting it up could be the better approach. This is especially true in lengthy surveys.

If you create a web form spanning multiple pages, users will want to know how far along they are in the process. You can indicate this in a variety of ways, such as:

- Progress bars indicating percentage complete
- Titles or headings indicating which step you are on and total number of steps
- Box navigation indicating where you are in the process
- "Next" buttons with meaningful titles (e.g., "Proceed to page 2 of 3")

So if you do choose to have a multi-page form, just make sure users understand what they are committing to by filling it out, and make sure they get indicators of their progress.

⦿ Making It Approachable

Invite People to Participate

While people need to fill out some forms in order to get a benefit (e.g., help from a librarian), surveys are usually optional. So you need to be extra conscientious in how you write surveys—and how you invite people to take them.

As you recruit participants, make a compelling case. Make it clear how the survey will benefit them. Perhaps your survey will:

- Provide valuable information to other library professionals
- Improve a library service they use regularly
- Make the community a better place to live

You might convince them it's a valuable survey, but people want to know if it's worth their time and effort. So be honest about how long it will take someone to fill out the form. Something with great value that only takes a few minutes is much more likely to be filled out than a twenty-minute survey with an unclear purpose (another reason to try and keep surveys short).

Use direct, active, and natural voice to better connect with your audience. Put your primary message first. Rather than saying, "On behalf of the library, I am requesting your participation in a data-collection effort," say something like, "We'd love for you to participate in our survey." If the invitation sounds complicated, readers will assume the survey itself is complicated and be less likely to fill it out. See table 9.2 for examples of improved language used to invite people to take surveys.

Table 9.2. Improved Survey Invitations

ORIGINAL SENTENCE	REVISED SENTENCE
This important data-collection effort is being undertaken to update the database.	We are doing this survey to improve our database.
The participation of community members across the county will ensure that all information contained in the system is accurate.	Your participation will ensure our information is up-to-date.
The city has authorized the Early Literacy Program, run by volunteers and administrators, to be made available to people in our community.	We're asking people in our community to fill out this survey so we can improve literacy among our youth.

Give It a Good Title

Use the title of a form to reflect its purpose. A well-articulated title can remove the need for descriptive or introductory text (which readers are likely to skip over anyway). For example, a description above a form that says, "Please fill out the form below to register for a field trip," is redundant if the title carries the same information: "Register for a Field Trip."

See table 9.3 for examples of improved titles of forms. Too often, form titles are several complicated nouns in a row, ending with the word *form*. Removing the word *form* (which is unnecessary) and translating the title into an action phrase will make it more approachable and direct.

Table 9.3. Form Titles Revised to Action Phrases

ORIGINAL TITLE	REVISED TITLE
Donation Submission Form	Donate to the Library
Reference Consultation Request Form	Ask a Librarian
Librarian Consultation Request Form	Request a Consultation with a Librarian
Profile Information Update Form	Manage Your Profile
Teacher Workshop Registration Request	Register for a Teacher Workshop

Surveys are a bit different, because they don't tend to initiate a task or interaction, but you can follow similar guidelines. The word *survey* isn't needed in the title and action phrases (beginning with strong verbs) still work well. For example, "Staff Professional Travel Planning Survey" is less effective as a title than "Share Your Professional Travel Plans." Remember that titles of surveys are especially important because they can convince participants to take them (or not). For surveys, consider starting with imperatives such as:

- Tell us . . .
- Share . . .
- Give us feedback on . . .
- Help us improve . . .

Treat It as a Conversation

Writing in general works best as a natural conversational style, but this is especially true when it comes to forms, since you are actually asking your users to respond to questions and participate in the conversation. Most of the time, it's best to keep your field labels succinct—and you can do so with common labels such as "Name," "Date," and "Phone number." But if there is a chance of ambiguity, a well-phrased question can make your intention crystal clear, avoiding confusion among your users.

Try to use language you would use in real life conversation. Consider a form to report a stolen library card. Rather than the field label "Issuing library," a more natural (and unambiguous) label would be, "What library gave you the card?" If a person is filling out their personal information, try using the label "Your name" rather than "Incumbent," "Affected party" or "Member name." If you have an open-ended input field for general comments, try simply using "Tell us more" rather than "Use the space below to provide detailed commentary and suggestions."

A good way to test the understandability of your writing is by reading it out loud. If you're building a form, find a nearby colleague and try reading the form out loud as dialogue, asking your colleague to respond to the questions. Do the questions flow easily and make sense? Is your colleague able to quickly interpret the questions and respond? Does it sound like a conversation between a friendly librarian and library visitor, or does it sound more like an interrogation? Approaching forms as natural conversations will go a long way to improving the user experience.

Key Points

Forms don't have to be so annoying. Strive for forms that are easy for readers to understand and complete. You'll get more accurate data, higher completion rates, and more confident end users. Remember:

- Only include what is necessary.
- Use a logical sequence and put instructions at the point of need.
- Follow conventions (there are lots of them).
- Make it action-oriented, direct, and unambiguous.

Forms are two-way conversations, and when written well, can build a relationship with your reader and lead to better interactions. This chapter has covered both print forms and web forms. Next up, we'll focus on the web in general and how to write intentionally with your web visitors in mind.

References

Jarrett, Caroline, and Gerry Gaffney. 2008. *Forms That Work: Designing Web Forms for Usability*. San Francisco: Morgan Kaufmann.

Wroblewski, Luke. 2008. *Web Form Design: Filling in the Blanks*. Brooklyn, NY: Rosenfeld Media.

Writing for the Web

WRITING FOR THE WEB IS A BIG, complex topic, and authors have written entire books on it. Most of the techniques outlined in this book are as relevant for the web as they are for print, but the web has enough unique attributes that it deserves special attention. In this chapter, you'll learn how people interact with web content and how to use this to your advantage.

Reading on the Web

People Want Information

People visit a particular website in order to achieve their goals. They want to either find information (gain knowledge) or complete a task (get something done). While the visual design of the website is important, it is the *content* that they care about most. This is undoubtedly true for library websites. Visitors don't tend to come to your library website for the joy of navigating or to see the latest homepage design. Rather, they want the information—the *content*. And they want it to be easy to find and easy to understand (Redish, 2012).

People Scan and Skim

When people are in a hurry, they will scan and skim content whether it is in print or on the web. But on the web, scanning and skimming is the default. Users are often busy and on a mission to get a particular question answered or task completed. They aren't interested in anything that isn't essential to what they are trying to do. As a web user yourself, this probably isn't surprising to hear. Even when on their final destination page, most users will skim and scan before they read.

Eye tracking studies have shown that users tend to scan website prose in an F-shaped pattern, focusing on words at the top left side of the page and then scanning for headings and keywords on the left side of the page (Nielsen, 2006). Users tend to pay the most attention to information at the top of the page, and tend to read at most 28 percent of the words on a page (Nielsen, 2013). This makes the words you use in your titles and headings especially important on the web—many times, the only thing users will read is titles and headings.

Write as a Conversation

As Janice Redish explains, good web writing is like a conversation (2012). People come to your website with a question and you answer it. Unlike other mediums, the web is interactive. Your web content talks directly to your site visitor, who then responds by interacting with links, filling out forms, and so on. As you write web content, think of the person calling you on the phone and asking you about the topic. Respond to him or her as if you were responding to an actual person on the phone.

If you pay attention to webpages and how content is written, you'll notice that most good web content is written in a conversational style. It's active voice. It's talking directly to the web user. It uses *you* to address you as the web user and *we* or *us* to talk about the organization.

Break Grammar Rules

In other sections of this book, you've been encouraged to relax and pay more attention to meaning and understanding than to grammatical details. On the web, this is even more important.

To improve the user experience, feel free to let go of a few rules. It's worth breaking a grammar rule if it improves fast comprehension (Loranger, 2014). On the web, it's fine to:

- Use sentence fragments
- Use numerical format for all numbers (not just ten and above)
- Have paragraphs containing just one or two sentences

NOT ALL PEOPLE ARE THE SAME

As with all content, think about your audience. Who visits your website? What are they trying to do? What is the context in which they are trying to do it? Pay attention to your users. Listen to how they describe things. Empathize with their mind-set and think in their vocabulary as you identify what questions they have when they visit your website. Not all audiences are the same, and you need to craft your writing around the people you are writing for.

ⓖ Focusing on Tasks and Essential Messages

Identify Primary Tasks

Whether building an entire website or a single webpage, try to identify the primary tasks of your audience. These can be written out as tasks or as questions. What are people trying to *do* on your website? In a public library setting, primary tasks might be:

- Searching for books, e-books, or films
- Finding library hours
- Registering for programs

You can also consider tasks as questions or information needs—what questions will your web content answer? On an academic website, these might be:

- How long can I check out a book?
- How can I submit a request for a book you don't have?
- Do you have laptops available for checkout and for how long?

By understanding the primary tasks and questions of your audience, you will better be able to prioritize content and write it in a way that makes sense.

CAN I USE ASTERISKS IN WEB WRITING?

As you try to focus on essential messages, you may be tempted to use asterisks to refer to supplemental content. But asterisks don't work well on the web. It's easy (usually) for your eyes to find the end of a print document where the asterisk is defined. The web doesn't have a similar visual "end" and often requires scrolling or navigating to a different page. When you are in the web environment, do not use asterisks. There is better technology (an advantage of the web), so you should be able to expand content or link out to definitions if needed.

Identify Trigger Words

Users trying to answer a question or complete a task will scan your content for keywords that will trigger them into clicking. Jared Spool (2004) calls these "trigger words." By including common trigger words, users are more likely to find the link that will get them closer to their goal. They are also more likely to find your content when they use those words in a search, so including trigger words in your content improves search engine optimization (SEO).

See table 10.1 for examples of trigger words for common library tasks. You can discover your users' trigger words through focus groups, user interviews, and by reviewing any search log data. It's helpful to be a librarian here, because this process is much like the process you would go through to identify concepts and keywords within a research topic.

Table 10.1. Examples of Trigger Words

USER TASK	TRIGGER WORD(S)
Do you have e-books I can download?	e-books
How can I get a library card? Can I apply online?	library card, application, apply
Can I rent a laptop from the library?	laptops, rent, rentals, borrow

---

CONTENT FIRST

Web design is an ever-evolving field, but a concept that's gained traction in recent years is a "content first" approach. This means that the most important thing to users is content. Content is what answers their questions and solves their problems, and so content should drive your design. No more *lorem ipsum*—or dummy content—in place of actual content. By dropping real content into a design, you get a much better sense of what the final output will be. When good, user-centered content is the priority, the design will not distract from it; it will highlight it.

Remember the Inverted Pyramid

The inverted pyramid was covered in chapter 3, but keep this technique in mind as you write individual webpages. Put the most important content first. For example, on a webpage about e-books, the most important message could be: e-books are available to download and here's how to find them. A secondary message could be: people can keep them for three weeks and renew them if there is no hold. The final message could be: you must have a current library card.

What questions would your users ask first? What is most important to their goals? What might they need to know next? And what will only a certain segment be interested in knowing? Most of the time, this is how you should order your webpage content.

Make Calls to Action Clear

Webpages are often stepping points to further action. Users often need to do something else to reach their goals. That next step is called a "call to action." What is the next step someone might need to take after reaching your webpage? Do they need to select a link to get to more information, or complete a form, or download a document? Identifying any call(s) to action at the outset will help you ensure these are made clear to the users through meaningful links, buttons, or other content. Be careful to make sure important calls to action are prominent and aren't hidden in paragraphs of text. Table 10.2 lists some examples of call(s) to actions on particular library webpages.

Table 10.2. Examples of Calls to Action

WEBPAGE	CALL(S) TO ACTION
Study rooms	Reserve a study room
Event page	RSVP for event
Borrowing information	Get a library card
Library account	Renew a book Update your profile

Avoid Fluff

Steve Krug (2014) wants to eliminate "happy talk" on websites—self-congratulatory fluff that contains little to no value to users. You'll often find happy talk on homepages, where organizations introduce themselves, sometimes providing a welcome message, mission, or vision statement. You'll also find it on individual webpages, where there is content introducing you to the rest of the content.

Similar to forms, there is rarely a need for an introduction. You shouldn't need to introduce your homepage or any webpage. A meaningful title, along with meaningful headings for skimming, should be sufficient. Users don't want to read, "Welcome to this library website!" They also don't want to read your mission statement. While there may be good reason to put your mission and vision statement, along with your strategic plan, up on your website for a particular segment of your audience, there is no need for it to be on the homepage. This type of fluff is unnecessary and adds minimal value. Table 10.3 has two examples of webpage fluff revised down to be more useful, succinct, and likely to be read.

Table 10.3. Revised, Simplified Homepage Copy

ORIGINAL	REVISED
This homepage of the library website provides access to the tools you'll need to find print, electronic, and multimedia resources in our library collections and on the web.	Find print, electronic, and multimedia resources.
The University Library Special Collections maintains collections of rare books and unique archival materials that make possible in-depth research on selected topics. The scope and diversity of Special Collections make it an important resource for the international academic community. Established in 1958 to house materials on the region, Special Collections now includes rare books, manuscript collections, photographs, and other materials in a wide variety of subject areas.	We offer access to rare and unique materials for scholars, researchers, and the public.

Keep Your Homepage Simple

The homepage is prime real estate, so everyone wants a spot for their thing. In an academic library setting, you might have twenty stakeholders with different priorities. Instruction librarians want it easy for professors to request instruction and for students to find research guides. Circulation staff want it easy to get to your account and renew books. Reference librarians want databases front and center, as well as a prominent spot for chat and email reference services. The marketing director wants news and events items as prime real estate.

If you don't have the primary tasks of your users identified, it can be challenging to prioritize content, or to turn down a stakeholder's request to have their things on the homepage. Even with the best intentions, your homepage can end up trying to accomplish too much, allowing your most important content to get lost. For the sake of your users, try to keep your homepage focused. Identify what the majority of your users want and need, and put that content in the forefront. Make it clear to stakeholders that not *everything* can be on the homepage, nor would you want it to be.

Balance Organizational Goals and User Goals

Websites serve many purposes and can help you reach organizational goals such as increased donations, increased attendance at events, and increased knowledge of your services and resources. That said, you need to be careful to balance your organizational goals with your users' goals. Don't let the goals of your organization trump the needs of your users. This can be a careful balance, and these goals can live together harmoniously. But focus on user goals first. For example, assuming your users' primary tasks relate to conducting research and finding materials, don't let the marketing department convince you that news and events information should have more homepage prominence than your search and discovery tools.

◎ Writing Links, Buttons, and Navigation Labels

Make Labels Meaningful

Users tend to visit more than just a single webpage—they will begin on one page of your website, then navigate around to the information they need. They might click through menus, links, or buttons to get where they need to go.

Clear, user-centered labels within your global menus as well as on links and buttons will make clear connections between content. It will make it easier for users to find the right path to answer their questions or complete their desired tasks. Jakob Nielsen refers to "information scent," where users select their navigation path based on cues, expecting a particular outcome. If your content has good information scent, users will be confident that they are headed in the right direction based on the links they are following. If it has poor information scent, users will likely be scrambling to figure out where to go next. They will find themselves hunting, or "foraging," for what they need with little confidence in ever finding it (Nielsen, 2003; Nielsen, 2004).

You likely have a primary, global navigation menu on your website. Menu labels make or break website navigation, so as you write these menus, try to keep them user-centered, parallel, succinct, and in a meaningful order. Focus on the task of your users and avoid jargon.

You also have links and buttons throughout your website, often within or adjacent to body text. As much as possible, use meaningful words that independently represent where these links will take you. Avoid labeling links simply "learn more" or "find out more." Without context, these have almost no meaning, causing poor information scent and bad accessibility (Sherwin, 2015). Even if surrounding text gives the link some meaning, "many users don't actually read the adjacent content and treat links as standalone items" (Pernice, 2014). By adding meaning to the link label, you'll not only make scanning content easier for everybody but also make it accessible to people using screen readers (who often scan through content to find links).

To make your labels most meaningful, use words that reflect where users will end up once they make the selection. Users should never be surprised by where a link takes them. The label should ideally match the name of the subsequent webpage, or should at least reflect the same content. Especially if you're linking people to a web form, try using the same wording as what you have on the title of the form so that users recognize they are in the correct, expected place. If the link says, "*apply for an internship*," users will expect the subsequent page to be an application for an internship.

Link labels can vary in length and grammatical style. They can be simple nouns, such as:

- To see what else is going on in the library, see *Library News*.
- Our computer lab has *printers and scanners*.

They can also be standalone phrases or full sentences, such as:

- *How to set up your preferences*
- *Renewing books and films*
- *See our strategic plan.*

While phrases and sentences are a good option, you do want to be careful to not overdo it, having long sentences that are hard to scan. Longer sentences can be particularly problematic on handheld devices, where they might take up two lines, causing readability problems.

Perhaps most commonly, especially when associated with tasks—links can be action phrases. These are often full (though short) imperative sentences:

- *Reserve a room*
- *Check room availability*
- *Apply for a locker*
- *Subscribe to newsletter*

Remove the Unnecessary

It should be obvious when something is a link or a button, so there is no need to use words like, *here, click here*, or *use this link to.* . . . If a link looks like a link, you don't need to call it out—people know how links work and understand that a click or tap action will take them somewhere else.

Similarly, you don't usually need to include the words *website* or *webpage*. Users expect that they will be taken to a webpage unless you tell them otherwise. That said, if the link

Table 10.4. Revised Link Labels

ORIGINAL LINK	REVISED LINK
The November/December Newsletter is *now available*!	The *November/December Newsletter* is now available!
Mentor applicants, please use this *form*. Mentees, please use this *form*.	*Apply to be a mentor.* *Apply to be a mentee.*
Click *here* and *here* to read recent reviews of the exhibition.	Read recent reviews: • *Library Exhibit Is Thought Provoking* • *Family Friendly Exhibition Is Worth Dealing with the Parking*
See our room availability web page for details on current availability.	*See room availability.*
If you are unable to find the book, *click here to go to Interlibrary Loan.*	If you are unable to find the book, use *Interlibrary Loan.*
Use this link to log into the registration system.	*Log into the registration system.*

goes to something else, such as a PDF file or other download, this can be worth indicating somehow (e.g., *"Employment Application [PDF]"*). See table 10.4 for examples of links revised to be more meaningful and succinct.

LINKS ARE EVERYWHERE

While this chapter is covering writing for the web, links can obviously be found beyond the web—in emails, documents, and presentations. No matter where you are putting links, the same rules apply.

Writing URLs

While some users won't see or pay attention to URLs, others will. And you might need to use URLs in print publicity or on digital signage. So try to keep them meaningful, short, and reflective of your website structure. The name of the URL should reflect the webpage it takes you to.

You've all seen those URLs you dread to type. Things like: https://www. professionalassociationexample.org/template.cfm?template=/WDApps/Committee/ appointingofficer/mycommittees. Imagine if all a reader has is a print version of a URL, such as in a list of references at the end of a book chapter, or that you need to put this URL on a poster. Lengthy and complex URLs are tedious and the readers are pretty much guaranteed to make mistakes when they try to type it.

When you have control over your URLs, keep them succinct. Don't include upper case, symbols, or punctuation. And use dashes (-) instead of underscores (_), since underscores can get lost if the URL is underlined.

ⓖ Writing for Search Results

When you search in Google—or any other search engine—you retrieve a list of results that includes webpage titles followed by descriptions. The descriptions are called "meta descriptions" and describe the content of each webpage.

When users don't like to navigate your website, or when they can't find what they are looking for by navigating it, they will search. As mentioned earlier, to make sure your webpages come up in search results, include trigger words in your content. But also pay close attention to the title of your pages and their meta descriptions, so that it is obvious what each webpage is all about and which webpages will get users closer to their goals.

Suppose a user searches your website for "lockers." In the results, the user sees a webpage titled "Lockers." A poor example of a meta description is "Lockers are approximately 17.25" deep, 9.25" wide, and 22.5" high. Library materials stored in the locker must be checked out. Food and drink are not allowed." A decent example of a meta description is: "The Main Library has 130 student fee-funded lockers available for currently enrolled students. They are located on the third floor." Both of these descriptions are useful in some ways, but they are also a bit verbose, overly detailed, and were just pulled from the content of the actual webpage (the default when you don't specifically write a meta description). A better, more succinct and active description is "Store your research materials in an assigned locker at the Main Library." Be meaningful and concise, because the intention is for the user to understand what the page is about and how it will get them closer to reaching their goal.

ⓖ Using Smart Structure

Layer Information

A nice feature of the web is you can easily layer information, hiding less relevant content until the point of need. This can be achieved through an interaction design technique called "progressive disclosure"—presenting only the content that's absolutely essential at that moment.

One way to do this is by offering a snippet of content about a topic along with an option to see more. This is a helpful technique for both drawing users in and for keeping your webpages focused and succinct. You'll often see this technique used for news and event content on library homepages.

Beyond the homepage, you'll also have pathway pages that are similar to a table of contents for a section of your website (Redish, 2012). They include links and often descriptions associated with those links. Users scan and select an option. A variation on pathway pages are research guides where librarians provide links to a variety of resources on a topic—usually resources that exist outside of the library website. Whatever the case, the descriptions of the options should include just enough information to let users decide if they want to make a selection.

So as you write snippets that lead to further content, keep in mind that you want to focus on what's important to your audience—what information will help them decide on whether the subsequent content or resource will be useful to their goals? For descriptions of databases, for example, you may want to include the type of content (e.g., scholarly articles, films, e-books) and the date range covered, but not a whole lot more.

Organize with the User in Mind

With primary tasks identified, a natural structure to the page might fall into place. For example, on a page about borrowing e-book readers from the library, you could have question headings written in logical sequence, in the order people would logically ask them:

- Who can borrow one?
- For how long?
- How can I check one out?

Alternatively, you might want to organize your content by time or sequence—this works well for processes. Or perhaps your content differs by audience, in which case you could break apart by audience type. This works well for borrowing information. However you choose to organize, do so with the user in mind.

Use Headings

On the web, headings have semantic meaning. Heading 1, or H1, should be hierarchically one level down from your title. Then sub-headings under H1 should be H2, subheadings under H2 should be H3, and so on.

As discussed in chapter 6, try writing headings as action phrases. Remember the power of parallelism, especially as many of your users will simply scan the headings on your webpage. Ginny Redish recommends two ways to write active headings on webpages: with gerunds (the form that ends in -*ing*) or with imperatives (the "do this" verb form). You can also use short questions for headings (Redish, 2012).

Use Bulleted Lists, Numbered Lists, and Tables

As described in chapter 7, you can use lists and tables to make content easier for users to scan and digest. Remember that tables work well for "if X, then Y" content. On your library website, try using tables for pricing information and circulation rules. Try using bullets for listing features of a particular service or tool. And try numbered lists for how-to guides and explaining a process.

BULLETS ALONE DON'T PROVIDE STRUCTURE

With good intentions, people often put bullets on a webpage, hoping this will make things easier to scan. But a list of ten or fifteen bullet points—in no logical order—is almost as difficult to scan as ten paragraphs. If you find yourself listing out a bunch of bullets, see if you can simplify content, group content, and break content apart more with headings.

Key Points

Writing for the web comes with its own challenges and opportunities. Remember:

- People aren't patient when they read on the web and have a particular goal in mind, so it's as important as ever to get to the point.
- Take advantage of technology to layer information, give the user control, and put content at the relevant time and place.
- Relax. It's the web.

The web is usually what people think of when they think of digital content, but you also write digital content as you interact with your colleagues, stakeholders, and end users. In the next chapter, you'll learn how to write better content for emails and other messaging systems.

References

Krug, Steve. 2014. *Don't Make Me Think Revisited: A Common-Sense Approach to Web and Mobile Usability*. San Francisco: New Riders.

Loranger, Hoa. 2014. "Break Grammar Rules on Websites for Clarity." Nielsen Norman Group. March 23. www.nngroup.com/articles/break-grammar-rules.

Nielsen, Jakob. 2003. "Information Foraging: Why Google Makes People Leave Your Site Faster." Nielsen Norman Group. June 30. www.nngroup.com/articles/information-scent.

———. 2004. "Deceivingly Strong Information Scent Costs Sales." Nielsen Norman Group. August 2. www.nngroup.com/articles/wrong-information-scent-costs-sales.

———. 2006. "F-Shaped Pattern for Reading Web Content." Nielsen Norman Group. April 17. www.nngroup.com/articles/f-shaped-pattern-reading-web-content.

———. 2013. "Website Reading: It (Sometimes) Does Happen." Nielsen Norman Group. June 24. www.nngroup.com/articles/website-reading.

Pernice, Kara. 2014. "A Link Is a Promise." Nielsen Norman Group. December 14. www.nngroup.com/articles/link-promise.

Redish, Janice. 2012. *Letting Go of the Words: Writing Web Content That Works*. San Francisco: Morgan Kaufmann.

Sherwin, Katie. 2015. "'Learn More' Links: You Can Do Better." Nielsen Norman Group. December 13. www.nngroup.com/articles/learn-more-links.

Spool, Jared. 2004. "The Right Trigger Words." UIE. November 15. https://articles.uie.com/trigger_words.

CHAPTER 11

Writing for Emails and Other Messaging Systems

Due to the prevalence of connectivity in daily life, digital, text-based interactions are a primary means of communication. It's common to have substantive conversations with colleagues through the written word, and threads over email and other messaging systems often take the place of in-person, spoken communication. So it's increasingly important to write well if you want to get any work done. In this chapter, learn how to best distribute information and have conversations through online systems, making your intentions clear and recipients aware of how to respond or act.

Why Email Matters

Even with today's abundance of tools for online messaging, email remains the most ubiquitous form of communication within organizations and businesses worldwide. Email is used daily to communicate with colleagues, supervisors, and subordinates, as well as clients, stakeholders, and end users. Good emails improve efficiencies, build relationships, and influence reputations.

Be Descriptive

Inbox overload is routine, and while some people might feel obligated to read emails you send them, most people have a choice. A strong opener is important in most forms of writing, but it's especially important in the world of email. So especially for those people you are trying to reach who don't *have* to open your email, it's important to think, "WWYO" or, "What would you open?" (Handley, 2014: 219).

Rather than read emails as they come in chronologically, people tend to skim over the subject lines, pre-headers, and sender information to identify which ones are most important or relevant at the moment. For each email, they quickly decide whether to read it, ignore it, file it to deal with later, or delete it. And deleting is often the most tempting of the options.

Your subject line is your first line of defense. So craft each subject line in a way that makes it clear what the email is all about and why the reader should care. Use the same practices you would use for writing a title, as covered in chapter 6. Be descriptive enough so your readers can make an informed decision on whether or not to open it (Nielsen, 2014), and in business writing, make sure your subject lines are as self-explanatory as possible (Canavor and Meirowitz, 2010).

Your colleagues and patrons should know what to expect when they open your email. See table 11.1 for examples of subject lines revised to be more descriptive.

Table 11.1. Ambiguous Subject Lines Revised to Be More Descriptive

ORIGINAL SUBJECT LINE	REVISED SUBJECT LINE
Meeting	Web redesign mtg minutes from 11/5
FWD: Article	Article about mental models
Update	Update on annual review process
Announcement	Announcement about upcoming retirement
Question	Interested in carpooling?

In addition to subject lines, pay attention to pre-headers (sometimes called "preview texts" or "snippet texts"). As people skim through their inboxes, they'll often see the subject line followed by the pre-header—a short summary line. Exactly what recipients see depends on their email client, but assume the pre-header is another piece of data that helps them determine whether or not to open an email. The default pre-header is the first line of text in the body of the email message. Especially if you are doing email marketing, pay attention to what appears in the pre-header, and consider customizing it (using HTML) to make it most useful and meaningful. Think of it as an extension of your subject line, and aim for forty to fifty characters to ensure it gets shown in full on most devices (Neely, 2015).

Make Subject Lines Brief

Aim for brevity. Subject lines should be six to ten words according to some studies (Handley, 2014), and no more than forty characters (Nielsen, 2014). Put the most important keywords at the beginning of the subject line, since some email clients will cut it off. And even if the subject line isn't cut off, many readers will only skim the first few words (Nielsen, 2014).

Use your limited space wisely. Be loose with your grammar, use abbreviations (if they are widely accepted), and feel free to omit articles (e.g. *the, an, a*) or other needless words. If you are sending out information on behalf of the library, and the library is obvious in the sender information, don't worry about including it in the subject line. See table 11.2 for examples of subject lines revised to be both meaningful and succinct.

Table 11.2. Subject Lines Revised to Be Brief Yet Meaningful

ORIGINAL SUBJECT LINE	REVISED SUBJECT LINE
Expert Search Services and Consultations on Research Strategies and Information Resources (89 characters, 11 words)	Providing In-Depth Research Help (32 characters, 4 words)
Tucson Public Library Announcement—Meet the New Library Director (53 characters, 8 words)	Meet Heidi Wiles—New Library Director (39 characters, 6 words)

Make It Personal

Libraries send emails to patrons to notify them of pertinent information, such as when materials are due. Ann Handley mentions that you are much more likely to get an email opened if you use the person's first name in the subject line (2014). For example, "Notice of Material Being Due" is much less compelling than "Your Book Is Almost Due, Shoshana." That said, some readers are wary when they see their name in a subject line, so do this carefully and in a way that builds trust rather than causes skepticism. If you make it personal, be sure to use only the first name, capitalize only the first letter of the name (never put it in all caps), and put it after the more meaningful content (Nielsen, 2014).

Use Common Acronyms

In work life, there are some commonly used acronyms that can help improve email efficiency. These are most often used in subject lines. Just be sure that others in your organization are familiar with them before using. For example:

- EOM = end of message (used at the end of a subject line to indicate there is no body content in an email). Example: "Out Sick Today EOM."
- FYI = for your information (used in subject lines or the body of an email to let readers know it is informational only—no response is expected). Example: "FYI— Coffee Shop Closing Early at 3 p.m."
- NWR = not work related (to let readers know it is a personal, rather than business, communication). Example: "NWR: School Fundraiser."

Keeping Emails Focused and Direct

Make Recipient(s) Clear

You'll generally start an email with a salutation, such as *Dear, Hi, Hello,* or *Hey,* followed by the name of the recipient(s). Use the salutation to help set the tone (see chapter 12) and to make it clear who you intend to read the email. Once you have more than three people on an email, it can be overwhelming to write out all their names. But when emailing a larger group of people, try to make it clear who is included. Perhaps you can say, "Dear ALA colleagues," "Hi Discovery Oversight Group," or "Greetings Mentoring Committee." This allows the reader to understand the audience and context of your message. If you are copying secondary audiences on the email, you can make this clear, too. For example, "Hello Search Committee (plus Glenda from HR)."

After an initial email, continuing to write out recipients' information is redundant and can add unnecessary clutter. But if there are multiple people on the email thread and you are seeking some response or action, make it clear *who* you want to hear back from. For example, "I'd love to get feedback from all committee members" or "Bonnie Jean, as the chair of the task force, let me know how you'd like to proceed."

NOT INCLUDING A SALUTATION

It is common to see emails that lack a salutation and simply address the person (or people) by first name. This has the benefit of reducing unnecessary words, but can also set an unfriendly tone in certain contexts. Be careful to not sound abrupt or hurried (unless that is your intention). If you are addressing a supervisor, for instance, using a salutation of *Dear* or *Hello* is more appropriate, at least for an initial email. If the conversation continues over the course of several messages, it's common after a time to remove the salutation. Follow social and organizational cues to make the best judgment call. And when in doubt, a salutation will never hurt.

Focus on Essential Messages

As a general guideline, try to have a single, clear purpose for each email. You'll find it's pretty easy and common to break this rule, and sometimes you can get away with it. Just be careful about putting *too* many messages in a single email, especially if they aren't related. Keep it focused and succinct, and make sure the first sentence indicates what you want the reader to *know* and/or what you want the reader to *do*. People are in a hurry when they are going through email and are often using their smartphone or other handheld device, so emails work best when they have an immediate purpose. People will "read quickly and distractedly—if you ask two questions in the same email, often you'll get a response to only one. Buried points and subtleties will also be overlooked" (Canavor and Meirowitz, 2010: 94).

WHAT IF I HAVE A LOT OF INFORMATION TO SHARE?

If you need to send something content heavy over email, try attaching it in a document rather than putting all the content within the body of the email. Formatting complex documents in email isn't ideal, and emails should always be short. Send bulky material as an attachment or link out to the document elsewhere, and treat the body of the email like a cover letter for the supplemental, content-rich material (Canavor and Meirowitz, 2010).

Make Intentions Clear

Do you want or expect a response to your email, or for the reader(s) to take some other action? If so, make that absolutely clear. Put it as either an imperative phrase (e.g., "Send me your feedback") or a question (e.g., "What is your timeline for . . . ?"). And if you have a deadline by which you need a response, make that clear, too.

Calls to action should be prominent at the beginning and/or end of your email, not in the middle and not hidden in a long paragraph. If you have a relatively simple message, try having a descriptive subject line and then putting the call to action first thing in the body of the email. For instance, you could have a subject line that reads, "Survey on Upcoming Travel Plans," and a first sentence in the body of the email that reads, "All library staff, please fill out *this brief survey* by the end of the week." Additional details about the survey—such as who is organizing it and how they plan to use the results—can follow.

FORWARD EMAILS WISELY

When you forward an email, make it clear why you are forwarding it. Simply forwarding something along without any context can frustrate the reader. Write a brief, meaningful sentence or two that explains why you are forwarding it. Avoid just writing, "FYI" or "Sharing FYI." Try something more like, "FYI—some interesting news from the state legislature we should all be aware of."

Sometimes, you'll need a bit more context beyond the subject line, and putting the call to action before the context won't make sense. In that case, put the context information first and the call to action last. For example, an email could read: "We are organizing a book sale and need volunteers in the coming weeks to organize, price, sort, and shelve books. We also need volunteers to staff the book sale on Saturday, June 19th. If you are interested in helping out, contact Ginger at (520) 555-7972." In this case, it wouldn't make sense to put the contact information first. The context is necessary for the contact information (the call to action) to make sense.

USE MEANINGFUL CAPITALIZATION

In work emails and documents, you will often find noun phrases capitalized as if they were proper nouns, when they really don't need to be capitalized. And as mentioned in chapter 6, capitalization worsens readability and should be used sparingly. If you are tempted to use title case, ask yourself, "Why?" Most of the time, you don't need to capitalize the names of documents, job titles, or form titles. Find out more about capitalization in chapter 13.

Use Active, Conversational Voice

When writing emails, you are literally having a conversation with your reader, so there is rarely an excuse for using passive voice. Take, for example:

> Dear workshop leader,
>   Workshop leaders are requested to submit their PPT presentation or other important materials for distribution to workshop attendees in print format.

This reads awkwardly because the writer is both using passive voice ("are requested") and using third person ("workshop leaders") to refer to the recipients. Whenever possible, address your recipients directly:

> Dear workshop leader,
>   Please submit your PPT presentation or other important materials so we can print and distribute them to workshop attendees.

As with all written communication, active, conversational voice is easiest for readers to digest. And this approach suits the email format beautifully, since it's intended for two-way (or multi-way) conversation.

Emails tend to be more informal than other forms of communication, so relax your style a bit. There is less of a need to be formal in tone, so avoid using phrases like "Please be advised that . . ." or "It is recommended that. . . ." Stick with more direct language, such as "Keep in mind that . . ." or, "I recommend that. . . ." Remember that direct, active phrases strengthen your message.

Organize

Organizing is simple when you have just a couple of sentences, but emails are often more complex than that. If you have more than two paragraphs of content, strategize on how to best organize it. When not much thought is put into organization, you can end up with redundancies or scattered content in no particular order, allowing your primary message or call to action to get lost. Take advantage of headings, lists, and tables as you would in other forms of writing (see chapters 6 and 7) to break up content and allow for skimming.

ⓖ Writing Useful Email Sender Information

Customize Sender Details

Most email clients allow you to associate details with an email address, such as a name and profile image. When someone receives an email, he or she can see the name along with any other sender details associated with that particular email address. Be sure sender details associated with your personal, professional, and organizational email accounts are accurate and useful. If you have multiple email addresses associated with your library, make sure each one has a meaningful name. For instance, ask@library.com could have the name "Ask a Librarian," and circadm@library.com could have the name "Library Circulation Department."

Sign Your Name

It's customary to "sign" your name at the end of an email. You can close with lines such as "Thanks/Thank you," "All the best," "Talk to you soon," or "I look forward to hearing from you." You can then choose to write your full name, your first name only, or just your initials. Your decision can affect the tone and provide a different level of information, so choose in a way that best reflects the goals of your message and your relationship with the recipient(s).

FOLLOW ORGANIZATIONAL NORMS

All work environments are different, so be sure to observe and reflect upon the culture of your own organization. Learn what is appropriate in email communication as far as tone, frequency, and topics covered. And adjust your approach based on your audience. Get feedback on emails you write, give others feedback on theirs, and try to foster a culture of effective online communication where email messages are appreciated as useful, not dismissed as a waste of time.

Include Signature Lines

Your email client can automatically add a signature line to the end of your emails, according to settings you customize. Signature lines should include useful information about who you are: your full name, title, organization, email address, and phone number.

But don't overdo it. A seven-line signature can be overwhelming. A good example of a signature line is:

Niamh Mayden
Undergraduate Services Librarian
University of Arizona Libraries
mayden@email.com
(520) 555-4934

A poorer, less focused example is:

Niamh Mayden, MLIS 2012
Undergraduate Services Librarian and Outreach College Coordinator
Chair, Committee on the Future of Publishing
Faculty Fellow Award Winner, 2016
University of Arizona
1510 E University Boulevard, Building #55
Tucson, Arizona 85712
mayden@email.com
Phone: (520) 555-4934
Fax: (520) 555-1501

It's generally not necessary to include your street address, fax number, or accolades. Stick to what is most important and useful for your audience. Feel free to customize your signature line by audience. For example, your signature line when communicating with other library professionals across the country might be different from when you communicate with clients or customers.

Including Links and Attachments in Emails

Presenting Links

Links were covered in the previous chapter in the context of writing for the web, but emails also contain links. The vast majority of email clients now support HTML emails, so treat your email content as you would your web content, allowing readers to scan content, navigate, and identify calls to action. See table 11.3 for examples of links within emails, revised to be more useful and accessible.

Unlike the web, you may want to occasionally spell out the URLs in your emails when it seems important for readers to understand exactly where a link is taking them.

Table 11.3. Revised Links in Email Messages

ORIGINAL EMAIL MESSAGE	REVISED EMAIL MESSAGE
I encourage you to read these posts *here*, and to share your ideas in your departments.	I encourage you to read *these posts* and to share your ideas in your departments.
See the attached call for proposals for full details and apply at *http://ose.az.gov/faculty-staff/apply-funding/* by March 15.	See the attached call for proposals for details and *apply on the OSE website* by March 15.

This is partly because of the prevalence of email spam where people have been taught not to trust links in emails for fear they aren't what they appear to be. Another factor is that links in emails aren't always to webpages, especially in the work environment. You might link your colleagues to documents in shared drives or forms on an intranet site, and you want your recipients to understand where you are taking them.

But URLs are still clunky and can clutter up your content, so this should be a last resort. Try first to just put context within the link title itself, such as *see the festival website* or *my draft in Dropbox*. If you are writing directly to colleagues, they will trust that you aren't linking them to something sinister. And if you are writing to your library users broadly, they should trust you based on your official email address and consistent dependability.

PROVIDE LINKS TO FILES, NOT JUST DIRECTIONS

In business emails, people occasionally tell you how to find a document rather than linking you to it directly. While it can be useful to include directions (depending on your audience), it is always helpful to include a direct link. So rather than writing, "The budget planning template can now be found in the Administrative Documents folder in a sub-folder names 'Budget Planning FY17,'" write: "Find the *budget planning template* in Administrative Documents > Budget Planning FY17." Recipients are much more likely to go to the document if you give them a direct link.

Describe Any Email Attachments

If you attach files to an email, make it clear in the body of the email that you've done so. And name the attachments something meaningful. Ambiguously titled attachments such as "upload" or "image" require the reader to look through the email to discover what the file is all about. This often isn't a big deal as it all depends on context, but do be thoughtful and intentional about it, especially if your audience is less familiar with the topic you are writing about.

A common email frustration is when the email subject line is vague (e.g., "Media Release"), the body is equally vague "FYI," and there is an attachment whose title is vague or redundant (e.g., "Media Release"). Recipients have to think, *What is this about? Is it relevant to me at all? Is it important?* Don't make your readers open an attachment with no notion of what content is inside. The curious might open it, but many will ignore it because it doesn't appear relevant. And if readers go to the trouble of opening the attachment and it turns out to be irrelevant, you've just lost some of their trust.

Using Email Marketing

Email is often used for marketing and promotions, where you aim to draw people to your library services, resources, and events. Some libraries use mass emails, sometimes called "email blasts," to promote events, share information, and solicit donations. These emails are mostly informational, so the techniques outlined in chapter 8 apply here. You'll also want to read chapter 12 to find out how you can bring in voice and tone into your marketing materials.

One of the best ways to make email marketing effective is to segment your audience. This allows you to make your messaging more relevant to the reader. For example, retired community members might be more interested in upcoming book sales, whereas parents of younger children might be more interested in new storytime offerings. Customizing and personalizing content will make your messages more focused and impactful.

One important writing convention related to email marketing is how you let recipients unsubscribe. While you might not want people to unsubscribe, making it clear how to do so will build trust with your readers. Follow the convention of putting this information at the bottom of the email and use the word *unsubscribe*. Be sure to write a meaningful link, such as "*Unsubscribe from this email list,*" rather than "To unsubscribe, click *here.*"

Chatting, Texting, and Other Messaging

Email is the classic form of online communication that has stood the test of time, but it's only one of many tools you probably use in daily life. You may use project management tools such as Asana, Trello, or Basecamp that allow you to track work and communicate across large teams. You also may be active within social media channels, such as Facebook, Twitter, and LinkedIn—all of which include their own private and group messaging systems. Whatever tool you are using, communicating via the written word in real time comes with its own nuances and challenges.

Chat or Text with Patrons

Many libraries offer a chat or text service, where the written word substitutes an in-person interaction. Unlike email, these conversations happen in real time, making it challenging since you don't get much time to think about how to organize and focus your content. But there are some things you can do to improve your writing in this fast-paced format:

- Use fragments and don't worry about capitalization and punctuation; just focus on getting your meaning across.
- Be honest, building trust with your users.
- Be friendly and approachable, using language you would use in person to avoid sounding rehearsed.
- Be quick and responsive, but not to the point of sloppiness.

Chat and text tend to be less formal than other types of communication. So feel free to say things like "Sorry, I'm slammed right now. Hang in there and I'll be with you in just a minute." This sounds more human and authentic than something like "Please hold for a few minutes. I will be able to assist you momentarily. I apologize for the inconvenience."

You may also use text to distribute information to individuals, perhaps notifying users when their interlibrary loan materials arrive, their books are late, or their accounts are expiring. These one-way texts can be a bit more formal than quick text responses might be, but should still be succinct. And if setting up text notifications for users, be sure to allow them to opt in or out, and give them an alternate option (such as email).

Chat or Text with Colleagues

You might have an instant messaging option at work, such as Skype for Business, that allows you to have real-time conversations with colleagues. You also may have communication tools (such as HipChat) that include a real-time chat feature. And you might even work in an environment where texting colleagues on their personal lines is commonplace. These can be great options when you want to ask quick questions or have short conversations. Use chat or text when you:

- Have a simple question
- Need a response quickly
- Don't need the conversation documented

Chat and text are inherently more casual than email. Tracking history is more difficult than email and is best used for short, informal conversations rather than for making important decisions or providing critical feedback.

Texting especially has a brief, often abrupt style by default. It is easy to sound rude when you are being short with words. So use text wisely. Texting your boss that you are late for a meeting is probably fine, but texting her that you are past due on your project report may be a bad move. Texting rarely fosters relationship building, and the shortness of text messages makes them difficult to relay context or deeper meaning.

Communicate in Forums

You also may have access to discussion forums with multiple participants. These tools often include advanced options such as creating specialized sub-forums, tagging individuals or groups, uploading or embedding files, and syncing with other productivity programs. Such forums are common in communities of practice as well as online or hybrid learning environments. So you might find yourself communicating in a Moodle forum with classmates, communicating with project teams in Slack, or communicating with likeminded professionals in a LinkedIn interest group. When using these types of forums, try:

- Focusing on one essential message per post
- Tagging specific people or groups if you want a response
- Using a meaningful title for your post (similar to an email subject line)

⊚ Key Points

Email has a bad rap, but you probably still use it daily to distribute information and get things done. Use email and other messaging tools thoughtfully to better communicate with end users and colleagues. Remember:

- Write good, self-explanatory subject lines, because people dislike emails and don't have to read them.
- Make your intentions and expectations clear, including any calls to action.
- Keep all messages focused and direct.

Most of the book so far has covered how to write for clarity. But there is more to writing than clarity—there is also creativity and personality. When writing to an external audience especially, you want to engage and inspire them, not just provide them with raw information. In the next chapter, you'll learn how to incorporate voice and tone across your messaging, and have a bit of fun doing it.

References

Canavor, Natalie, and Claire Meirowitz. 2010. *The Truth about the New Rules of Business Writing.* Upper Saddle River, NJ: FT Press.

Handley, Ann. 2014. *Everybody Writes: Your Go-To Guide for Creating Ridiculously Good Content.* Hoboken, NJ: Wiley.

Neely, Pam. 2015. "How to Write Better Preheader Text in Your Next Email Marketing Campaign." *Campaign Monitor* (blog). August 12. www.campaignmonitor.com/blog/email-marketing/2015/08/improve-email-open-rates-with-preheader-text.

Nielsen Norman Group. 2014. "Email Subject Lines: 5 Tips to Attract Readers." Nielsen Norman Group. May 4. www.nngroup.com/articles/email-subject-lines.

Implementing Voice and Tone

IN ADDITION TO SHARING INFORMATION with your readers, your writing can stimulate their imaginations, stir up their emotions, and inspire their thinking. Writing allows the reader to get to know your personality and style—as an individual or as an organization. What are the values you live by? What keeps you up at night? Are you casual and quirky, or polished and academic? In this chapter, learn how to implement a personal and organizational brand that is meaningful, compelling, and unique to you.

Finding a Balance

Commit to Clarity

By now, you recognize the importance of clarity in writing. And after focusing on the power of plain language, you may be skeptical about bringing in a dose of creativity. How can you write in a way that is vivid and memorable when your focus is on keeping things as brief and articulate as possible?

Creativity should never undermine clarity, so your goal is to find that sweet spot. Unproductive adjectives, adverbs, and modifiers are bad. But compelling adjectives and adverbs can add flavor and actually enhance clarity in your writing. You can (and should) get imaginative. Just be intentional about it and do it *only* when it serves a purpose.

BE CAUTIOUS WITH IDIOMS

As you get more creative with your writing, you'll be tempted to use idioms—words and phrases not to be taken literally. These should be used sparingly, especially if your audience includes nonnative speakers. Common idioms include "in a nutshell," "jump on the bandwagon," and "best of both worlds." Idioms can be fun, but you can see why a nonnative speaker might be confused by them.

Be Engaging

Without sacrificing clarity, try adding graphic language to paint mental images for your readers, spark their imaginations, and bring your point home. Natalie Canavor recommends you "engage the senses" (2016: 72) by thinking of terms that reflect things you see, hear, feel, and smell. Try using not just active verbs, but also *graphic* verbs that bring ideas to life. You could just articulate the facts: "Our reading room has lots of windows, comfy furniture, and an outside view." Not bad, but something a bit more descriptive allows readers to imagine themselves in the space: "Our reading lounge is surrounded by large windows and drenched in natural light. Sink into our sofas and gaze out at the lush green countryside while relaxing with your favorite book." Notice the senses—readers can *feel* the sofas and *see* the view through the windows.

Selecting descriptive, vivid words enhances your writing and brings your voice to life. Also try writing stories, placing content in a human context, and using (clear!) analogies to achieve the same goal.

Be Empathetic

As you work to refine content and cut unnecessary words, beware of oversimplifying things to a point where voice becomes nonexistent. In the better cases, oversimplified content can come off as abrupt. In the worst cases, it can lead to trouble and misunderstanding, especially in the workplace. So while you should strive for clarity, you should also show respect, empathy, courtesy, and appreciation for your readers. In an email to an employee who you supervise, for instance, you will do better spending a few extra words to indicate your appreciation for their hard work. So rather than saying simply "The report is due Friday at noon," you could say, "As you know, the report is due Friday at noon. I appreciate all your hard work on this, and let me know if you need any guidance in the meantime."

USING HUMOR IN WRITING

Everyone loves to laugh, but be cautious when using humor in your writing. Be sure you have a really good sense of your audience so that something intended to be funny isn't interpreted as offensive or judgmental. Irony and sarcasm are especially problematic. Comedy is a tough craft to learn, so test out any humorous moments in your writing with some readers to gauge their reactions before putting them out there to the world.

⑯ Implementing Your Personal, Professional Voice

Your Voice Is an Asset

Simply put, your voice is who you are. It reflects your personality and point of view, and is what makes your writing unique. A strong, approachable, sincere voice helps you convey ideas, build trust, influence others, and get things done. Being intentional about your written communication style will lead to deeper relationships with your colleagues as well as job advancement and career growth.

You might write a dozen emails in a day, but don't underestimate their importance. Natalie Canavor suggests you "use every [email] message to present yourself in the way you want to be seen. In fact, because email is so important to the everyday business flow in nearly every organization, it's a stellar chance to continuously showcase yourself and impress others" (2016: 13–14). See table 12.1 for examples of how a slight adjustment in voice can alter how you feel about a particular email message.

Table 12.1. Content Revised to Reflect Approachable Voice

ORIGINAL CONTENT	REVISED CONTENT
QUESTIONS? Ask me.	Please be in touch if you have any questions.
Apply before the deadline!!	Apply by Friday, June 3rd, for first consideration.
The decision to consistently post salary ranges on all job postings was driven by your feedback via the survey.	Thanks to everyone for providing thoughtful input via the survey! Because of your feedback, we will now post salary ranges on all job postings.

Define and Refine Your Current Voice

You already have a voice behind your writing, whether you're aware of it or not. Every message you write conveys subtle emotions and insight into your personality, for better or worse. Reflect upon your current voice and strive to build and improve on it.

How would your supervisor or colleagues describe your writing? For example, would they say you appear "confident" (usually a good thing) or "overconfident," which can be interpreted as aggressive or pushy? Start to define your voice by listing out adjectives you imagine others would use to characterize your writing style. Everyone has blind spots, so ask some trusted colleagues to contribute to and provide feedback on your list.

Next, refine your unique voice by writing "[adjective], but not [adjective]." The "X, not Y" method is recommended by Kate Kiefer Lee, content curator at MailChimp (2012a), and also advocated by Halvorson and Rach in *Content Strategy for the Web* (2012). Pull out the positive descriptors from your list that you want to build upon, and then contrast them with the things you don't want to be. For example:

- Direct, but not rude
- Decisive, but not stubborn
- Thoughtful, but not tentative
- Fun, but not childish

- Casual, but not unprofessional
- Courteous, but not a pushover

Once you've defined your ideal voice, find a handful of things you've previously written to see how well they meet the criteria. And then spend a little extra time on upcoming, important communications to best reflect your defined voice—perhaps a grant proposal, cover letter, or performance evaluation.

Be Original and Compelling

Content often gets lost in a sea of information, so a fresh and unexpected voice helps you stand out from the crowd. Reflect your authentic self in your writing. Perhaps you are calm under pressure, and you demonstrate this with the graceful way you present in front of large audiences or facilitate difficult conversations. Or perhaps you are quirky and lighthearted, and it shows in the way you provide comic relief during long meetings or tangent to personal anecdotes during project updates. Whatever the case, *own* it. Embrace your individual personality and reflect it in your writing style. As long as it doesn't hinder your communication, it tells your story. It makes you memorable and distinctly you.

Keep this in mind when you apply for a job, promotion, or award. Your cover letter is a chance to express your unique voice and story, and it can set you apart from other applicants. The days of academic, formal letters are slowly coming to an end, as employers seek people with creativity, enthusiasm, and individuality.

USING EMOTICONS AND EMOJI

Since facial expressions and body language don't exist in the written word, we have emoticons and emoji. These can express happiness, confusion, anger, and even love. Whether or not to use these symbols in your written communications is a personal decision. They can make you more personable and approachable, but could on the other hand make you seem less professional, especially in some contexts. A good rule of thumb is to use emoticons or emoji in personal, informal writing, but avoid them in more professional or business communications.

◎ Implementing Your Library's Voice

Your Library's Voice Is an Asset

Your library's voice reflects the personality of the organization and the people within it. A unique, approachable, authentic voice will distinguish your library from the competition. It will also inspire trust and confidence in your readers, and build relationships with them over time.

Define and Refine Your Current Voice

Your voice should reflect your organizational identity. As a library organization, what are you passionate about? What is your vision for the future? What is the bigger story you are trying to tell about who you are and what you do? Ideally, your content at all levels should consistently reflect that larger organizational identity and message.

> ### KNOW YOUR MISSION, BUT FOCUS ON YOUR READERS
>
> While your content should *reflect* your library's goals, be sure to focus on the reader, not the library. Readers don't want to learn what the library is all about, just why the library should matter to them. They wonder, "How can the library help me?" not, "Tell me all about the library!"

So how do you identify and document your library's voice? Some libraries have a defined brand already, and this is a good stepping stone to having a defined voice. Defining a unique voice is challenging, but is also a good opportunity for self-reflection and reinvention. Facilitating dialogue across your organization on this topic can lead to better articulation of your library's identity, values, and vision.

To be successful, your voice has to be supported by your library's leadership. Margot Bloomstein (2012) suggests a card-sorting exercise with your top administrators. For this activity:

1. List out a few dozen adjectives on note cards. This can be anything from *friendly* and *innovative* to *traditional* and *wise*. If you already have an established brand, include terms that reflect that brand.
2. Ask administrators to place the cards into one of three categories: "who we are," "who we'd like to be," and "who we're not." Allow them to add new adjectives that aren't yet captured.
3. As a group, discuss and analyze what was placed where and why.

At the end of the session, you should have a good sense of the messaging your administrators would like to see. To get a more complete picture, conduct a similar exercise with members of your actual audience, using the three categories: "the library is," "the library should be," and "the library is not." Then pull all the data together and draft guidelines for your voice and tone based on what you *are* and what you *aspire to be*. As mentioned earlier, the format "X, but not Y" works well. For example:

- Reassuring, but not paternalistic
- Inspiring, but not cheerleady
- Academic, but not highbrow
- Fun, but not funny
- Carefree, but not careless

Be Original and Compelling

Get creative as you write about your library's unique collections, services, and people. Use graphic language that inspires the senses and keeps readers invested in what you have to say. Perhaps you are promoting your film databases during the summer months. Rather than a Facebook post simply saying, "Film databases available on library website," try something more descriptive like "Access thousands of movies at your fingertips! When it's too hot to be outside, stream a foreign, classic, or documentary film in the comfort of your own home."

Experiment, also, with adding a bit of mystery to your content. Imagine describing the storage room where you keep rare books, and one of your goals is to build support for their long-term preservation. Intrigue your readers with content such as: "Our steel-enclosed vault can withstand the force of a bulldozer. At a crisp 50 degrees Fahrenheit, we keep it cool, dry, and sterile. The only sound in this isolated, closed vault is the faint buzz of our dehumidifier. It might not be a place to spend a romantic evening, but it's a perfect home for our rare materials, such as our handwritten manuscripts, rare books, and aging photographs. These materials will stand the test of time as long as we keep them in these highly controlled conditions."

Tell Stories

Seek out and share stories that include human issues and emotions. Storytelling is especially powerful when you're encouraging people to donate money or volunteer time. For example, a donor may have a story about how your archive brought his family history to life and deepened his relationship with his parents. Or perhaps there is a researcher who used materials to move forward a project that's improving the lives of young entrepreneurs around the globe.

Even in small doses, storytelling can add character to your content and engage your readers. See table 12.2 for ideas on how to take something basic and bring it to life with a story.

Table 12.2. Content Revised to Tell a Story

ORIGINAL CONTENT	REVISED CONTENT
Write an essay for the chance to win $1,000.	Take a $1,000 vacation after hitting the books all semester. All you have to do is write an essay.
The program supports graduate students both financially and through library work experience. *See the video* for student interviews.	The program has supported dozens of graduate students, who not only receive financial support during their studies but also have the opportunity to gain real-world experience working in the library. In this *video interview*, alums share how Kate's gift made their studies easier and gave them practical experience needed in their future careers.

Implement across Channels

Ideally, your library's voice should be reflected in all content written by library staff and shared with the world. This probably includes a myriad of employees writing webpages, Facebook posts, job advertisements, event invitations, signage, and email notices, to name a few.

Implementing a consistent voice across a library (especially a large one) is no small task. To start, document voice standards and guidelines. In this documentation, define your voice and examples of how to apply it. Include:

- At least three sets of adjectives in the form of "X, but not Y"
- Examples of messaging that doesn't fit the voice along with revised messaging that fits the voice well
- A list of terminology to use and not use (see table 12.3)

It's also helpful to write up a set of content principles. Such principles can set a foundation for the way people will approach any writing project. For example:

- It's all about the user, so use second person (*you*) more than first person (*we*).
- Make the user feel smart.
- Less is more.

Table 12.3. Examples of Voice and Tone Guidelines

DON'T USE	INSTEAD USE
Awesome	Amazing
Hey	Hello
Sincerely	All the best
Don't forget to	Try not to
Never	Be careful to not

With voice guidelines in place, you can then conduct training sessions, establish editing workflows, and develop methods of accountability. You might need a handful of trained reviewers to provide feedback on new content, or regular meetings with content creators to ensure your voice is remaining consistent. Your marketing or user-experience unit would likely play a key role in overseeing such a process.

CLARITY FIRST

While it serves you well to bring a unique, fun voice to your library, be careful to not get carried away. Storytelling and analogies can be great fun, but don't sacrifice clarity for wittiness.

Ⓢ Adapt Your Tone

While your voice should remain consistent, your tone can (and should) change based on the context. For instance, content promoting a literary award might be more cheerful than content on library fines or a code of conduct. You can still be concise and helpful (your voice), but your tone will differ (more or less serious, more or less funny). As Kate Kiefer Lee points out, "Our voice makes us unique, and our tone makes us sound like humans" (2012a). Use tone to express empathy with users and their situations.

So while your personal, professional voice might be fun, sometimes you'll need to tone down the "fun." In an email recognizing a colleague you might say, "Congrats—you are a rock star!" but in a rejection letter you might say, "Sadly, we aren't able to offer you the position at this time. We had a blast getting to know you and appreciate all the time you spent with us. We wish you the best of luck in your search." It's not appropriate to use exclamation points or hyperbole in a rejection letter, though it could be perfectly appropriate in a congratulatory letter. In this example, the voice hasn't changed—it comes from the same unique perspective—but the *tone* has changed.

How do you determine tone? Consider your reader(s), your relationship to your reader(s), and the topic at hand. If you are writing an email and know the readers, consider their personalities and how they might receive your message. For example, maybe it's okay to be opinionated and decisive if it is what your readers need and anticipate. Your relationship to the readers also plays a role—your tone when writing to a close friend ought to differ from that used to write to someone you've never met before.

Finally, consider the topic of discussion and the goal of your message. If it is a serious goal (such as getting the person to apologize for a mistake), the tone should match that intention. If it is a lighthearted topic, such as inviting people to a scavenger hunt at your library, an upbeat tone could fit the bill.

DELIVERING BAD NEWS

Communicating bad news through the written word is a hard thing to do, and requires special attention to tone. Be straightforward, making sure nothing is ambiguous. Provide context for the news, such as why a particular decision was made. And be sure to show compassion for those affected by the news, whether it is the reader or others. If you can and it's appropriate, include additional information or guidance the reader might find helpful. For example, if you are telling an applicant they did not receive a job offer, you can share other related opportunities they may want to consider. If you are telling a library patron they owe money in replacement book costs, you can let them know about flexible payment plans or other alternate options.

Getting Creative and Keeping It Interesting

Explore Word Choice

There is no single *right* way to say something, and the English language provides immeasurable options for the resourceful writer. Allow your thesaurus to become your close, personal friend. For inspiration, read and study a variety of writing styles, from science fiction to political journalism. Expand your vocabulary, get creative, and experiment with word choice and ordering. Tinker, adjust, and adapt.

Pay Attention to Rhythm

A bunch of similarly constructed sentences in a row will bore your readers, so mix it up. Read aloud and recognize the sound and rhythm of the written word. Alternate the length and structure of your sentences so they carry different weight. Keep it interesting. Don't let your readers zone out to the hum of a monotonous writing style.

Take Some Risk

There are mechanics to writing, and you'll benefit from understanding rules of grammar and usage. But these rules are fluid and change over time, so feel free to take a bit of risk. If you think your readers will be receptive, throw in a bit of slang, wittiness, or gentle humor and see how they respond. Try switching things up, perhaps by turning nouns into verbs (e.g., "Let's lunch") or using less conventional structures, like a sentence containing just one noun or one verb. Also experiment in your approaches to the writing process, breaking away from your normal routine to inspire new ideas and ways of thinking.

Taking risks can pay off in a big way by engaging new audiences and making more memorable impressions. And in today's digital world, you can usually go in and edit something when it doesn't work out. So you can relax, learn from your experience, and just do things differently the next time. Most importantly, have fun with it.

◎ Key Points

Voice and tone bring life to your content. Remember:

- Clarity is a priority, but creativity is good, too.
- Build upon your unique voice to engage readers and build relationships.
- Experiment and have fun with it.

Now that you know the fundamentals of writing well, it's time to talk details in putting it all together. In the next chapter, you'll learn some tricks related to formatting and design.

◎ References

Bloomstein, Margot. 2012. *Content Strategy at Work: Real-World Stories to Strengthen Every Interactive Project*. Amsterdam: Morgan Kaufmann.

Canavor, Natalie. 2016. *Business Writing Today: A Practical Guide*. Los Angeles: Sage Publications.

Halvorson, Kristina, and Melissa Rach. 2012. *Content Strategy for the Web*. 2nd ed. Berkeley, CA: New Riders.

Lee, Kate Kiefer. 2012a. "Tone and Voice: Showing Your Users That You Care." *UX Magazine*, September 17. http://uxmag.com/articles/tone-and-voice-showing-your-users-that-you-care.

———. 2012b. "Warby Parker's Honest Brand Voice." *Forbes*, September 19. www.forbes.com/sites/katelee/2012/09/19/warby-parkers-honest-brand-voice.

Leibtag, Ahava. 2013. *The Digital Crown: Winning at Content on the Web*. Waltham, MA: Morgan Kaufmann.

Rocket Science Group. 2016. "Voice and Tone." Accessed July 23. http://voiceandtone.com.

Formatting Your Content

EVEN THE BEST-WRITTEN CONTENT can fail if it's poorly designed on the page. In this chapter, you'll learn how to best display words on a page (or screen) by using space effectively, selecting fonts carefully, and making sensible formatting decisions.

Making Content Accessible

Use Semantic Markup

Titles and headings, as discussed in chapter 6, play critical roles in both setting the stage for your message and organizing your content. And they shouldn't just *look* like titles and headings, they should be *marked up* as such, whether it is through HTML (e.g., <title>, <h1>, <h2>) or through built-in styles available in most text-editing programs. Semantic markup of titles and headings is especially helpful for visually impaired people accessing your content through screen reader programs such as JAWS (Freedom Scientific).

All major word processing and presentation software programs allow you to use semantic heading structure. They provide you with default title and heading styles, but let you customize them to whatever styles you like, whether it's by modifying styles in your toolbar in Microsoft Word or formatting master slides in Keynote for Mac. And if you convert to PDF format, you can translate the marked-up headings into "bookmarks," a comparable option.

Readers can then view outlines of clickable headings or bookmarks alongside your documents, similar to navigation menus on websites or tables of contents in books. These outlines allow readers to easily review a document's structure and navigate to different sections. Readers will especially appreciate this detail if they are working their way through long-form documents or handbooks.

While semantic markup is most relevant for titles and headings, it's also useful for attaching other meaning to words, such as emphasis (<em> or <strong>) or quote (<blockquote>). Explore your editor and use semantic styles to make sure any meaning you want conveyed to readers is marked up properly.

Use Color Contrast

Font and background color play a key role in legibility of content. Black text on a white background is a safe bet, but if you're creating a slideshow, flyer, or website, you'll likely want to get a bit more creative.

Fortunately, color contrast analyzers are freely available online through such sites as WebAIM (2016) and Paciello Group (2016). If you're writing for digital presentation, be sure to check body content as well as titles, headings, buttons, and links. And keep in mind that the presentation of colors can differ across operating systems, browsers, devices, and monitors. So even if something appears to have good contrast on your screen, it may not be as distinctive for all readers. Using a tool to check for color contrast is your best bet.

Format for Color-Blind Readers

About 5–8 percent of men have some form of color deficiency and cannot distinguish red or green (Redish, 2012). As you select font colors, background colors, and graphics, consider this population and avoid attributing meaning to colors, especially with shades of red and green. To see what your content or images look like for people who are color blind, run a simulation—there are many simulators available freely on the web.

USING BACKGROUND COLORS IN EMAIL

Background colors and graphics in email are problematic. Not only do they reduce legibility for the intended recipients and sometimes not even display properly on their screens, but also the background often transfers over when people then respond to or forward the message. And if their default font color doesn't match that of the original message (which is usually the case), it can become even harder to read. Imagine forwarding an article to a colleague along with a note about why she should read it, but that note comes out as blue font on a purple background—which is incredibly hard to read. Avoid this problem by sticking with the default white background on all email messages. (This includes marketing email blasts and newsletters. Even if it looks pretty when sent out, it could be problematic when forwarded.)

Strive for AAA Conformance

The World Wide Web Consortium, more commonly known as W3C, develops web standards for accessibility. W3C is behind the detailed Web Content Accessibility Guidelines (WCAG), which explain how to make web content accessible to people with disabilities. The guidelines are organized under four principles: perceivable, operable, understandable, and robust (Henry, 2012). A Triple-A, or AAA, level of conformance means your content meets all criteria for accessibility.

Needless to say, you should strive for your content to meet the AAA level. That said, this high level of conformance restricts your design options and can be tough to achieve (for example, you can't use color to draw attention to links), so AA might be sufficient. Explore the WCAG 2.0 requirements and techniques at www.w3.org/WAI/WCAG20/quickref. Know your audience, conduct testing, and when in doubt, favor accessibility over flashy design.

⊚ Using Space Well

Use White Space

White space is the empty space between and around content. White space is an active part of any design, so use it and place it deliberately. Not only does it make your work readable and easier to comprehend (Handley, 2014; Fadeyev, 2009), but it also frames text and makes divisions and sections more clear (Ross and Nilsen, 2013). It also indicates relationships and hierarchy between pieces of content.

Put Space between Content

Avoid the dreaded wall of text by sprinkling white space intentionally throughout your content. Use short paragraphs organized under meaningful headings (see chapters 4 and 6). When it makes sense, include tables, graphics, and bulleted and numbered lists (see chapter 7).

Be generous with the amount of space between lines, called *leading* (rhymes with *sledding*) in the field of typography. Ensure you have plenty of spacing not just between one body line and the next, but also between paragraphs and between items in bulleted or numbered lists.

Include plenty of padding within your table rows and columns so that text is never squished next to the borders inside a table cell. If you are using charts or graphics, make sure there is a good amount of buffer surrounding them. Avoid having wrapper text appear tightly next to a graphical element. Every element will benefit from a bit of breathing room.

Put Space around Content

Use white space to frame your content, too. When writing letters and reports on traditional 8.5 × 11-inch paper, leave generous margins of 1.25 inches (Ross and Nilsen, 2013). When designing a webpage, don't have text take up the full width of the computer screen. Make it easy for readers' eyes to go from one line to the next without losing their place.

◉ Selecting Fonts

Use No More Than Three Fonts

Your best bet is to pick one good font in a readable size and stick with it, especially if you are just writing an email message or simple report. Two and occasionally three fonts are acceptable when designing something a bit more complex, like a website or brochure. But once you get past three fonts your message is almost guaranteed to appear unprofessional or chaotic.

Use Serif and Sans-Serif Fonts

Serifs are small counterstrokes at the ends of the main strokes in an individual letter. Times New Roman, Garamound, and Georgia are serif fonts, because they have counterstrokes. Calibri, Arial, Helvetica, and Verdana are sans-serif, because they don't have counterstrokes.

You have a choice between serif and sans-serif fonts, and what's best can depend on whether you are creating content for a digital medium (like a website) or for print (like a poster). What's best also depends on whether it's for paragraph-style content or just short snippets of text, like headings and titles. As a general rule, when producing content for digital presentation, use sans-serif fonts for body text and serif fonts for titles and headings. For high-resolution print documents, use serif fonts for body text and sans-serif fonts for titles and headings (Ross and Nilsen, 2013). This is not a hard-and-fast rule, but it is a useful guideline.

Pay Attention to Letter Spacing

When you select a font, pay attention to the space between letters and between words. In typography, this is called *letter-spacing*, *character spacing*, or *tracking* (not to be confused with *kerning*, which applies to spacing between a particular pair of characters). Fonts with poor letter-spacing tend to be more tightly connected, causing readability issues. If you find a font you like but the words appear cramped, you can always use letter-spacing to customize to your liking. You can also use tracking for particular purposes, such as headings written in all caps that appear dense by default and would benefit from a bit of extra spacing.

Select a Standard Font Size

Ensure the size of your font doesn't hinder readability. For your body text in documents and emails, 12pt is standard for most fonts. You can go down to 10pt for certain fonts (like Verdana), but avoid going any lower than that. On the web, it's much more complicated, given the ability for font sizes to respond to devices and browser sizes, but you can assume the equivalent of 12pt is 16 pixels (Pamental, 2014).

Pick an Appropriate Font Color

Aim for consistent font color(s) that look crisp against your chosen background. If you're working on a plain white (or off-white) background, dark grays, blues, and browns tend to be easy to read. Reds, yellows, oranges, and light colors are much harder to read. If you have colorful graphics or imagery in the background, you might be challenged to find a font color that works well. Again, use a color contrast checker to make sure your content is accessible.

You might be tempted to highlight particular words using different colors, but try to avoid using more than one font color within your body content. On the web, this can make words look like links when they're not. Some colors can be hard on the eyes and reduce legibility, and color-blind readers may not notice the colors at all. Unless you're a skilled designer, the safest approach is to use the same font color for both headings and body content, and avoid using color to try and convey meaning.

Also be cautious of using colors that carry some connotation. The color red—often innocently used for emphasis—will infer a sense of seriousness or urgency even if that isn't the intention. And people often assume the color blue indicates a link (Fadeyev, 2009). So rather than using font color to draw attention, try using **bold**.

EMPHASIS

People often try to emphasize a particular piece of content through some combination of bold, italics, exclamation points, all caps, and bright colors. It's common to see "*IMPORTANT!!*" or "*PLEASE NOTE*" in bright red on webpages or in training handbooks. Avoid falling into this trap. Not only can this method hinder your content's readability and accessibility, but it can hurt your credibility as well. This type of messaging looks less professional and can appear as if you're shouting at or talking down to your readers. There are usually better options. Try using just **bold**, or ordering content more thoughtfully, or cutting things down to your essential messages, or using an alternate option to bring focus to a piece of content such as sidebars and callouts.

Aligning Content

In most cases, left align your content: flush left, ragged (rag) right. It is the most readable alignment because it provides uniform letter and word spacing, minimizes awkward hyphenation of words, and provides the eye with a common starting point for each line.

Justification of text is one alternate option where each line adjusts to a uniform length, giving you straight edges on both the left and right side of your content. While it may create a clean, symmetrical presentation, justified text causes readability issues due to the uneven character spacing. You also often end up with a plethora of hyphenated words. Never use justified text on the web, since it's a flexible, fluid environment that doesn't like the constraints of justification (Cousins, 2013). The only time where you may want to justify text is for important, formal, printed documents—perhaps your strategic plan brochure or code of conduct poster where it's important that you convey an official tone.

Centered text should also be used with discretion, as people have a hard time reading it. It's ragged left and ragged right, and forces readers' eyes to zigzag throughout a paragraph of content, continuously searching for the start of the next line (Redish, 2012). This is much more tiring for the eyes than left-aligned text. The only times centered text works is when it is a title, a heading, or just a few words. But even in these cases be cautious. Menu items in web navigation, column headings in tables, and short lines of text within tables are easier to skim and scan when lined up on the left.

Right alignment of text (flush right, ragged left) is similarly problematic, forcing the reader's eye to move even more to find the start of the next line. Right alignment should be a rare occurrence, only used for small blocks of text or artistic elements (Cousins, 2013).

Using Capital Letters, Italics, Underline, and Bold

Avoid All Caps

You should rarely, if ever, use ALL CAPS in your writing. Capitalized letters take up more space, slow reading speed, are boring, are harder to read, and make it seem like you're shouting (Redish, 2012).

You might be tempted to use all caps to bring emphasis to just a word or two, for example in a form label "Your name (REQUIRED)" or in calling out new information, as in "UPDATE." You also might want to use all caps to indicate sections within your content or to call attention to your email subject line. Avoid this urge. Instead, try:

- Using conventions (e.g., an asterisk for a required form field)
- Using sidebars or call-outs to draw attention to updates or important information
- Using bold to emphasize particular words
- Formatting headings using bold, color, and/or a larger font size
- Writing useful headings and having a clear structure to the content
- Putting the most important content first
- Using powerful language that stands on its own (no emphasis required)

In other words, there is usually an alternative to all caps. The only time it's acceptable to use all caps is as a design decision for your titles and headings, and even then only if you keep your titles and headings to just a few words. For instance, the short title "RE-QUEST ITEMS" is readable, but the longer title "REQUEST BOOKS, ARTICLES, DISSERTATIONS, AND MEDIA ITEMS" is much harder on the eyes. And some argue that even in titles and headings, using all caps is never a good choice (Redish, 2012).

Use Title Capitalization Sparingly

Title capitalization has its time and place, but as talked about in chapter 6, it can make things a bit harder to read and should only be used when useful or necessary. You might be tempted to use title capitalization for any "official" term, but usually these aren't true proper nouns and capitalization isn't necessary. For instance, it's perfectly fine to use sentence case for:

- Job titles (e.g., dean of the library, graphic designer)
- Library services (e.g., interlibrary loan, technology lending)

- Processes and policies (e.g., performance review cycle, professional development policy)
- Projects and initiatives (e.g., signage project, digital collections revamp)
- Groups of people (e.g., web team, subject librarians)
- Buildings or places (e.g., library, fifth floor)
- Buzz words (e.g., content marketing)

That said, it is best to use title capitalization for true proper nouns, such as your university name, library name, and officially named spaces or tools:

- University of Arizona
- University of Arizona Libraries
- Russo Quiet Study Room
- Guide on the Side

Creating a style guide or editorial standards that identify which common words to treat as titles and which to put in sentence case will improve overall readability and consistency.

Avoid Underlines

Underlining also causes readability and usability issues. Since the beginning of the web, people have been taught that underlined words are links. So on the web, the *only* thing ever underlined should be links. If something is underlined and it isn't a link, users will certainly assume that it is (Canavor, 2016; Redish, 2012).

Even when writing for print, be cautious about underlining. Bold or italics are usually a better choice, because words become harder to read when underlined. And there is a good chance your print document will be digitized, since few things exist in only print format these days. Unless you need to underline something for a very clear reason—such as formatting within a citation—it's best to just avoid it.

Use Italics Sparingly

Italics, similar to **bold**, are often used for emphasis. But as most things, they can be overused or used inappropriately. Italics make things harder to read, and so italicizing a sentence of text, or even worse—a paragraph of text—can make it significantly harder to read (Redish, 2012). So when using italics, use it only for a word or two, and only when it serves a clear purpose.

ONE SPACE AFTER PUNCTUATION OR TWO?

Back in the day of typewriters, people were taught to put two spaces after a period or other punctuation. Some people continue this tradition, but it is no longer useful for readability and can actually distract the reader. It's also a common inconsistency. Keep it simple by always using just one space after punctuation.

⟲ Key Points

You can have the best content in the world but will frustrate your readers if you fail to pay attention to formatting. Remember:

- Your content should be accessible to people of all abilities.
- White space is your friend and gives your content breathing room.
- Standard fonts, left alignment, and sentence case are best.

There is just one chapter to go. In the next and final chapter, you'll learn tips to improve your writing process from start to finish.

⟲ References

Canavor, Natalie. 2016. *Business Writing Today: A Practical Guide.* Los Angeles: Sage Publications

Cousins, Carrie. 2013. "The Importance of Designing for Readability." *Design Shack.* July 22. https://designshack.net/articles/mobile/the-importance-of-designing-for-readability.

Fadeyev, Dmitry. 2009. "10 Useful Usability Findings and Guidelines." *Smashing Magazine.* September 24. www.smashingmagazine.com/2009/09/10-useful-usability-findings-and-guidelines.

Handley, Ann. 2014. *Everybody Writes: Your Go-To Guide for Creating Ridiculously Good Content.* Hoboken, NJ: Wiley.

Henry, Shawn Lawton. 2012. "Web Content Accessibility Guidelines (WCAG) Overview." Last updated October 2. www.w3.org/WAI/intro/wcag.

Paciello Group. 2016. "Colour Contrast Analyser." Accessed July 15. www.paciellogroup.com/resources/contrastanalyser.

Pamental, Jason. 2014. "A More Modern Scale for Web Typography." Typecast by Monotype. January 15. http://typecast.com/blog/a-more-modern-scale-for-web-typography.

Redish, Janice. 2012. *Letting Go of the Words: Writing Web Content That Works.* San Francisco: Morgan Kaufmann.

Ross, Catherine Sheldrick, and Kirsti Nilsen. 2013. *Communicating Professionally: A How-to-Do-It Manual for Librarians.* 3rd ed. Chicago: Neal-Schuman.

WebAIM. 2016. "Color Contrast Checker." http://webaim.org/resources/contrastchecker.

Refining Your Process

Throughout this book, you've learned techniques to improve your writing, but there is no one right way to write. Explore different approaches and processes to find what suits you best. Adjust, adapt, experiment, and seek out ways to continually improve your writing over time. In this chapter, you'll learn how to put everything together and think through the entire process of writing.

⟲ Dedicating Time and Energy

Take It Seriously

Writing can be a lot of fun. But writing in a way that is clear, focused, and engaging isn't easy to do. More often than not, it's time-consuming and stressful. You may stare at a blank screen and fear you'll never be able to come up with the right words. You may spend twenty minutes struggling over a couple of words that just don't sound right. You may get frustrated and delete the whole thing and start over. Writing well is hard, and if you really want to improve your writing, commit to taking it seriously and taking the time to do it right.

Set Time Aside

Learning to write well takes time and patience. Don't expect to master the craft of writing by just reading a book or two. And don't expect to become a better writer with just a little bit of practice. It takes *a lot* of practice. Intentional, daily practice.

So if you're serious about becoming a better writer, set some time aside. This could be just a half hour at the end of every work day to read and rewrite sloppy content you wrote in the past. Or a four-hour block one Friday a month to reflect on your recent writing successes and challenges. Put it on your calendar so that you stick to it. You don't have all the time in the world, but you should be able to squeeze in just a bit of time—scheduled, focused, uninterrupted time dedicated to improving your craft.

Set Goals

Come up with some practical, measurable goals for yourself or your library. The pure act of documenting goals will keep you motivated and more likely to follow through. These goals will be most useful if they both improve the experience for your readers as well as give you practice improving your writing. For example, you could aim to:

- Remove all jargon from building signage
- Cut your website content in half
- Improve your email response rate by 50 percent

After establishing goals, give yourself a deadline or—for more complex goals—a timeline that includes significant milestones toward the goal. When you succeed in a goal or significant milestone, recognize and celebrate that success.

Be Patient

Writing can be frustrating. There's a lot to think about: make sure your writing is simple but not choppy, compelling but not complex, and unambiguous but stripped down to the essentials. Achieving this can be a real struggle, and it's often a matter of finding balance between all the things you're taught.

Be patient and kind to yourself. Don't get stressed out when you hit writer's block or can't seem to find the right words. Even the most highly trained and experienced writers still share in these struggles. Writing is always going to take time and effort. Get through it by practicing patience, flexibility, and persistence.

COME BACK TO IT

Occasionally, you'll find yourself going crazy over a single sentence (or paragraph). You keep rewording it, but can never get it quite right. If you find yourself in this type of situation and you're getting worked up over it, just put the content aside for a bit and come back to it later. Even if it's just for a few minutes. It's often easier to evaluate and improve upon a sentence after looking at it with fresh eyes.

Practice

The only sure way to improve your writing is through practice. Commit to a continued, intentional writing practice. And seek out opportunities to exercise and fine tune your writing skills. If a colleague is writing an important report, offer to edit it. If you don't understand an email message the first time you read it, try to make sense of it through a rewrite. If you receive a letter from the electric company that seems overly complex, try revising it with the audience in mind. It takes effort, but jumping on these opportunities as part of your daily routine will make you a better, more conscientious writer over time.

⊚ Planning (Up to a Point)

Know Your Readers

As discussed in chapter 2, you should know your audience and write with your audience in mind. Don't begin writing without at least a vague understanding of who will be interpreting your message. For smaller projects, try writing this out at the top of your draft as a constant reminder of who you are writing for. For larger projects, create a planning document that includes a detailed description of your audience, perhaps even breaking them into primary and secondary audience segments.

Define Your Message(s) and Purpose

As discussed in chapter 3, a fundamental step to any writing project is defining your goals. This includes both your readers' and your organizational or personal goals. Having these goals in mind will keep you grounded and focused. They will also help you best organize your content.

Again, for smaller projects you can experiment with putting this information at the top of your draft. For larger projects, try documenting a plan that explicitly identifies the:

- Primary message(s)
- Readers' goals and motivations
- Organizational (or personal) goals
- Calls to action

The articulation of these elements will keep you focused and on message.

Outline Your Ideas

With your readers and goals in mind, you'll probably find it helpful to then outline your ideas. An outline will help you organize your thoughts. Try experimenting with a variety of formats to see what works best for you:

- A rough sketch of your primary messages in priority order
- A list of content chunks that seem like they might go together
- A visual mind map that gathers and connects your thoughts
- A structured outline of titles and headings

Whatever the case, a drafty outline of the entire content tends to be a better starting point than trying to jump in and write everything out in a linear fashion (at least for larger projects).

Get Something on a Page

Whether it's an outline or a written stream of consciousness, getting something down on a page is the first step, and is often the hardest part. Ann Handley (2014) calls it "The Ugly First Draft," or TUFD. It can be sloppy, childish, and even nonsensical much of the time. But that's okay, because it's just the beginning. You'll be rewriting it, probably many times.

Be Flexible

Writing is an iterative process, not a linear one, so you can only plan so much. Don't be tied to a set outline or plan. As you begin to put content on the page, you'll often find that your original plan won't work out so well. For example, the original outline for this book was thirteen chapters; it's now fourteen. More than half of the chapter titles are not what were listed in the original outline. Some chapters expanded in scope and length, and some became more focused.

As Zinsser writes, "Don't ever become the prisoner of a preconceived plan. Writing is no respecter of blueprints" (2006: 53). The writing process is full of surprises and you can't anticipate how things will go, so stay flexible and adapt to what you discover along the way.

◎ Revising Your Writing

Revise Everything

Professional writers don't have magical powers allowing them to write perfectly on first try. In fact, experienced writers rarely write something just once. Canavor argues that no matter who the writer, "the first version is usually awful" (2016: 66). But the first thing you write is always just the first draft. *Expect* to edit it. As Zinsser explains, "Rewriting is the essence of writing. . . . Professional writers rewrite their sentences repeatedly and then rewrite what they have rewritten" (2006: 4). Professionals do it and you should do it, too. Rewrite every email message, every brochure, and every conference proposal. Reread it, and then edit it. Then do it again. And again. Until you have it just right.

Reach Out to Others

Another set of eyes is always useful. Identify a trusted colleague with an editing background, a passion for writing well, an attention to detail, and/or a knack for telling you like it is. When you invite someone to give you feedback, make it clear what you're asking for. Feedback on your grammar is far different from feedback on the substance of the content itself, and you may want different people to give you different types of feedback.

Read It Aloud

As discussed in chapter 5, your writing should flow as naturally as the spoken word. So read it aloud. Notice what sounds authentic and approachable, and what sounds mechanical and impersonal. Ask:

- Does it sound like something you'd say in person?
- Is there a nice rhythm to the sentences (or do they sound choppy or long-winded)?
- Do you have transitions where they're useful to help with the flow?

It's an incredibly basic technique, but reading your writing aloud is a quick, easy way to discover what's working well and what still needs some work.

PRINT IT OUT

When writing something in long-form, like a report or article, try printing it out to review it in a different medium. You absorb text in print differently than text on a screen, so it's likely you'll see things jump out at you that you didn't previously notice. Bring some pens to mark up your print copy, crossing things out and moving things around. Try using standard copyediting marks (such as carets [^] for inserts) for consistency, so that you'll understand your meaning later on.

Review for Substance and Clarity

The substance and clarity of your content is key. Keeping your audience and goals in mind, ask:

- Is the content timely and relevant?
- Is there an obvious focus?
- Is the primary message clear?
- Are any calls to action clear?
- Is anything ambiguous?
- Is anything unnecessary?
- Are you using common patterns and conventions?
- Does the content address readers' motivations?
- Does the content reflect organizational or personal goals?

Be ruthless in your critique. Rewrite words and sentences until they are crystal clear. Cut words, strip down sentences, and remove anything that doesn't serve a function. Replace adverbs with stronger verbs, jargon with plain language, and passive sentences with active ones. Replace wordy instructions with numbered lists, run-on sentences with bulleted lists, and sets of "if, then" statements with tables. Keep tinkering. There is almost always another thing to improve on.

Review for Voice and Tone

Review your content to ensure it consistently reflects your defined voice (see chapter 12). Then evaluate if the tone aligns with the situation.

If you're getting creative with your language, seek an outside perspective to make sure you're on the mark. To evaluate your voice, try conducting an exercise where you ask readers to circle descriptive words based on their experience. Use adjectives both within and outside of your defined voice and see what rises to the top. Is the content fun? Boring? Cheesy?

If you're dealing with a sticky situation, you'll want to make sure you get the tone just right. This can be hard to judge on your own, so try to find a person or two willing to give you feedback, focusing on how content makes them feel. It's worth the extra effort to ensure you don't unintentionally damage a relationship.

KEEP AN OPEN MIND

It can be hard to receive criticism, but as you solicit feedback, be sure to listen to it closely, take it seriously, and avoid becoming defensive. Try to be objective about your own writing and keep an open mind to others' suggestions.

Review for Audience

Remember your intended audience, including their motivations and challenges. Make sure you are speaking in language that resonates and is relevant to their world. Don't use jargon your audience doesn't understand or content not applicable to their goals. When in doubt, track down someone from your actual audience who can look over your writing and provide you with feedback.

Review for Flow and Structure

Your content should have an obvious, logical structure that allows people to both read it and navigate through it seamlessly. Ask:

- Is the most important content first?
- Does the ordering make sense?
- Are the headings parallel?
- Are transitions used well?
- Is there rhythm from one section to the next?
- Is there a good mix of sentence structure?
- Are bulleted and numbered lists used appropriately?

For longer documents with a good number of headings, review the headings from top to bottom and make sure they have a coherent flow. If your content is within a larger context (such as a website), review it with that larger context in mind.

PERFECT THE OPENER

Your opening few lines set the stage for the rest of your content, so spend the time and effort to get them just right. Zinsser advises, "I urge you not to count on the reader to stick around. Readers want to know—very soon—what's in it for them" (2016: 55).

Review for Spelling and Grammar

Errors in spelling and grammar are unprofessional, and can distract and confuse your readers. Use automated spelling and grammar checks in your editing program, and get further support with free tools such as Grammarly and the Hemingway App. But remember, such tools don't catch all subtle mistakes and can occasionally "correct" things for you erroneously. Human editors are still the most effective, so ask someone to proof your work, especially if you're prone to typos and grammatical errors.

> **PROFESSIONAL EDITING**
>
> Getting everything right is no small feat, and you might not have skilled writers at your beck and call. You can also become so immersed in your own writing that it's hard to stay objective. So for your most important writing, consider hiring a professional editor. As Stephen King says, "To write is human, to edit is divine" (2000: 13).

Take a Breather

When you've revised as much as you can for now, walk away. Let your writing sit for a few hours or even a day or week or more, depending on its importance. Come back to it with fresh eyes. Without exception, you will notice something you want to change when you look at it again.

> **THERE'S NO TIME!**
>
> No doubt, time is a commodity. So in many instances you simply won't have time for detailed review and revisions. That's okay. If you are on a short deadline, consider the smallest thing you can do to improve upon your writing, even if it's just reading your email aloud once or twice. If you have an extra minute, try to remove any unnecessary, fiddly words. Or try improving upon your title or subject line. Even minimal changes can have a big impact to the reader.
>
> The revision process for larger content projects will always require significant time. But as most things, revisions will become quicker and easier with practice. Effort and persistence will pay off.

⑥ Evaluating Your Writing

Identify Success Measures

Ideally, you want to know whether or not your content was successful in meeting your goals. To do this, try exploring possible measures. For digital content, look at analytics data, such as referral paths, conversion rates, and bounce rates. Track how long it takes someone to read over content and make a decision or complete a call to action. If you are curious what content is most relevant, use heat mapping or eye tracking to discover where people focus their attention on a webpage. If you are revising content, experiment with pre- and post-assessment to see the impact of your change.

By setting up metrics for content, you can identify areas of strength and opportunities for improvement. You can also use this data to demonstrate the value of good content.

Conduct Usability Testing

Usability testing is a way to evaluate a product's usability by observing actual people trying to use it. Good content is core to a product's usability, so try applying usability testing methods to evaluate how well your content is working.

If your content is on a webpage, you can test its effectiveness by asking participants to find an answer to a question or complete a task on your website. All you have to do is incorporate a task that aligns to the content on the webpage. Be sure to ask participants to think aloud and share their impressions, either as they go (the "thinking aloud" method) or after the fact ("retrospective review" method) (Blakiston, 2014).

Content outside of websites can be tested using similar methods. For instance, you can test content within brochures by prompting participants to find answers to particular questions within them. See table 14.1 for more examples of how to test different types of content using different types of prompts.

Table 14.1. Prompts for Testing Content with Real People

TYPE OF CONTENT	EXAMPLE OF PROMPT
Event registration form	Register for the event using this form.
Steps for setting up an account	Follow these written instructions to set up your account.
News story	Read this article and summarize for me what you learned.
Directional signs	Try to locate the children's books based only on the signage in the building.

Once the participant completes the activity, it's helpful to dive deeper into his or her experience. This additional qualitative data will help you identify problematic content and provide you with ideas for improvement. Consider asking participants such questions as:

- How easy or difficult was it to understand?
- How much of it would you say you read?
- What words stood out to you?
- If you were to paraphrase the purpose of this content, what would you say?
- What did you learn that you didn't know before?

Use what you learn to identify areas for improvement.

Interview Your Readers

Another method to evaluate content is to simply talk to your readers and gather their impressions. As you frame your questions, be careful they are neutral and don't lead respondents in any particular direction. For example, don't say, "Isn't that funny the way we wrote that?" Rather, say, "What do you think about the way we wrote that?" Some other useful, open-ended questions are:

- What do you think about the content?
- How did it make you feel?
- What did you learn from it?
- What did you like about it?
- What did you not like about it?

Again, use what you find out to identify the content's strengths and weaknesses; then make improvements.

Refining Your Craft

Focus on Clarity of Thought

It can be challenging to write in plain language if your thoughts are scattered, since writing is an emotional process driven by what's going on in your brain. Focus your thoughts, and focused writing will follow. Practice mindfulness. Remove distractions from your environment. Identify quiet, calm places (both physically and mentally) where you can do your best writing.

Improve Your Vocabulary and Grammar

Expand your vocabulary through deep reading, listening, and a drive to keep learning. If you hear a new word, look it up. A greater breadth of vocabulary will allow you to express your thoughts in an infinite number of ways.

This book didn't talk much about grammar (there are many other books for that), and it's a moving target as language continues to evolve. But that doesn't mean it's not important. If you don't already have it, acquire a basic, rudimentary understanding of grammar so that you can write meaningful content. Once the basics are in place, consider ramping up your knowledge. It will make you a better reader, writer, and communicator. And when a proofreader fixes your grammatical error, be sure to learn from it and avoid it the next time.

Read and Observe

Become a better reader and you will become a better writer. Read deeply and analyze what you're reading. Good writing can inspire you, and bad writing can help you avoid similar mistakes. You don't have to read a novel a week, but you should dedicate focused time on a regular basis to sit back and read something—anything—whether it is your favorite cooking blog, a popular entertainment magazine, or the latest bestseller.

Also be curious about the world around you, observing content of all types you encounter throughout the day, from restaurant menus to parking garage signage. If you notice a piece of content you don't like, analyze it to identify its pitfalls. Does it have too many adverbs? Is it ripe with passive voice? Is it trying to convey too many messages? Is it formatted poorly? Once you've identified what's wrong with it, imagine how you might rewrite it.

As colleagues work on their own writing projects, offer to provide feedback or play the role of editor. Seek out others who are passionate about the written word and team up to improve content together. Get comfortable reviewing and providing feedback to other writers, as well as soliciting feedback for your own work.

Spreading the Word

You Can't Do This Alone

There is a good chance that you are not the only voice behind your organization. You might have marketers responsible for news stories and social media, graphic designers responsible for signage and brochures, subject librarians responsible for web content, and public services staff responsible for email and text notices. How on earth can you implement a consistent approach to writing across your organization when there are so many players? It's not easy, but there are some things you can do.

To start, identify colleagues who also value good content. Form a group of like-minded writers committed to improving communication both inside and outside the library. Strategize about how you can work together to improve the clarity, consistency, and overall quality of writing across the organization.

Create a Style Guide

Advocate for a detailed style guide for all your public-facing content. This will encourage consistency across communication channels, no matter the author. Your style guide should include audience definitions, voice and tone examples, and terminology preferences. It can also include such rules as:

- Use conversational language.
- Use active voice.
- Put essential messages first.
- Explain any jargon.
- Avoid acronyms.

Your style guide can also ensure consistency of formatting with such rules as:

- Use sentence case for headings.
- Avoid all caps and underlines.
- Use lowercase for job titles.
- Use title case for department names.

If you work in a university or corporate setting, your parent organization may already have a style guide. So be sure to identify any existing standards (often managed through marketing) and work them into a guide specific to your library setting.

Conduct Training Sessions

Establish a training program for all employees who write public-facing content. Training sessions can cover the topics in this book along with voice, tone, and style decisions specific to your library.

If a dozen content providers write for your website, create a training program specifically on writing for the web. If all your subject librarians create LibGuides, put together workshops on writing instructional and descriptive content specifically for research guides.

Develop a Content Strategy

To sustain quality content over time, you need to manage the entire lifecycle of content throughout your organization, from first draft to publication to deletion. This is where the discipline of content strategy comes in. A thoughtful content strategy will allow you to establish roles and responsibilities, governance structures, standards, workflows, and methods of accountability. Halvorson and Rach's *Content Strategy for the Web* (2012) is a brilliant overview, and you can also read case studies on how the University of Arizona Libraries has made headway in this area (Blakiston, 2013; Blakiston and Mayden, 2015). Indeed, knowing how to write succinct, meaningful content is wonderful, and this book has given you advice on how to do just that. But it is only the beginning—now you need to go out in the world, continue to build up your skills, and spread the love for good writing throughout the library profession.

◎ Key Points

Improving your writing takes effort. Continue to expand your toolbox and refine your craft over time. Remember:

- Writing well is hard work, so take it seriously (up to a point).
- Some planning up front will make things easier later on.
- Writing is a craft. Hone your craft.

◎ References

Blakiston, Rebecca. 2013. "Developing a Content Strategy for an Academic Library Website." *Journal of Electronic Resources Librarianship* 25, no. 3: 175–91.

———. 2014. *Usability Testing: A Practical Guide for Librarians.* Lanham, MD: Rowman & Littlefield.

Blakiston, Rebecca, and Shoshana Mayden. 2015. "How We Hired a Content Strategist (and Why You Should Too)." *Journal of Web Librarianship* 9, no. 4: 193–215.

Canavor, Natalie. 2016. *Business Writing Today: A Practical Guide.* 2nd ed. Thousand Oaks, CA: Sage.

Halvorson, Kristina, and Melissa Rach. 2012. *Content Strategy for the Web.* 2nd ed. San Francisco: New Riders.

Handley, Ann. 2014. *Everybody Writes: Your Go-To Guide for Creating Ridiculously Good Content.* Hoboken, NJ: Wiley.

King, Stephen. 2000. *On Writing: A Memoir of the Craft.* New York: Scribner.

Zinsser, William. 2006. *On Writing Well: The Classic Guide to Writing Nonfiction.* New York: Harper & Row.

Index

accessibility, 59, 75, 94, 107–8, 135–39. *See also* screen readers; readability

acronyms, 16, 43, 116, 152

active verbs, 50–51, 56–57, 61

active voice, 41, 47–*49*, 83, *98*, 102, 118

adjectives, 32–33, 36, 50, 125

adverbs, *32*, 36, 50, 125, 147

all caps, 79, 115, 138–40, 152. *See also* capitalization

ALT text, 107. *See also* accessibility

ambiguity, 36; emails, 114, 121; forms, 90, 94, 99; policies, 5, 42; signage, 78, 81; titles, 55–56, 78; verbs, 86

analogies, 126, 132

analytics. *See* web analytics

ARI. *See* automated readability index

asterisks, 31, 93–94, 103, 140. *See also* footnotes and endnotes

audience, 11–18, 43, 46, 54–5, 102–3, 120, 122, 145, 148. *See also* donors; faculty; personas; students

authenticity, 41–42, 51, 56, 128, 146–47

automated readability index, 37

Baron, Naomi, 7, 22

Blakiston, Rebecca, 150, 153

blogs, 5, 22, 25, 54, 59

Bloomstein, Margot, 129,

bolding text, 86–87, 139, 140, 141. *See also* emphasis; italicizing text

Brandon, John, 79

brochures, 77–78; text alignment in, 139; asterisks in, 31; fonts, 138; examples of, 2–3, 22, 24–55; testing with readers, 150; titles of, 26, 53–54

Bruckman, Amy, 82

bulleted lists, 65–66, 70–73, 73, 87, 112, 127

buzzwords, 36, 45, 50, 130

calls to action: defining, 17, 24–25; placement of, *26*; reflecting in emails, 117–18; reflecting in titles, 56–57; reflecting in webpages, 104–*5*

Canavor, Natalie, 18, 31, 34–36, 38, 114, 117, 126–27, 141, 146

capitalization, 54, 118, 140–41. *See also* all caps

CAPTCHA, 95

centered text. *See* text alignment

Chapman, C.C., 45, 47

charts. *See* figures

chat, 122–23

check boxes, 89, 94, 111. *See also* forms; radio buttons

Coleman-Liau index, 37–38

colloquialisms, 46. *See also* idioms

colons, 57–58, 66, 93

color contrast, 136. *See also* accessibility

communication channels, 5–6, 13, 131–32, 152

compound sentences, 70, 87

concept nouns, 49

conjunctions, 46

consistency, 54, 64–*67*, 71, 86–87, 93, 129, 131, 152. *See also* parallelism

content first, 104

content strategy, 169

contractions, 46

conventions, 93–94, 122, 140, 147

copyediting. *See* editing

Cousins, Carrie, 139–140

cover letters, 117, 128
creativity, 3, 80, 125, 128, 130, 133–134

dashes, 31, 42, 45, 109
deep reading, 7, 151
dictionary, 42–43
discussion forums, 123
donors, 14, 24, 54, 91, 131. *See also* audience
drop–downs, 64, 89, 94–95, 111. *See also* forms; menus

e-books, 7
editing, 43–44, 146, 149, 152
emails, 4, *114, 115, 120*; background colors, 136; email marketing, 114, 121–22; pre–headers, 114; signature lines, 119–20; subject lines, 26, 50, 56, 58-59, 114–18, 121, 123, 140
emoji, 128
emoticons, 46, 128
empathy, 11–12, 14–15, 18, 102, 126, 132
emphasis, 136, 139–40. *See also* bolding text; italicizing text
endnotes. *See* footnotes and endnotes
English as a second language. *See* nonnative speakers
error messages, 95
eye tracking, 102, 150
exclamation points, 46, 79, 132, 139
exhibits, 3, 6, 54, 60, 62

Facebook. *See* social media
faculty, 13, 15, 22, 27, 74. *See also* audience
Fadeyev, Dmitry, 137, 139
false series, 66
FAQs. *See* frequently asked questions
field labels, *92*–94, 99. *See also* forms
Fiesler, Casey, 82
figures, 75
first drafts, 162
first person, 43–44, 67, 84, 131
Flesch-Kincaid, 37–38
flow, 32, 45, 59, 66, 147–48
flyers, 1–3, 54, 77–78, 136. *See also* brochures
focus groups. *See* user research
fonts, 79–80, 136, 138–39
footnotes and endnotes, 28, 31. *See also* asterisks
formatting, 135–42. *See also* accessibility; capitalization; fonts; text alignment; white space
forms, 89–100, *98. See also* check boxes; field labels; help text; radio buttons

fragments, 46, 122
frequently asked questions, 3, 27, 63
Fry readability formula, 37
fun, 44–47, 78, 80, 127, 129–130, 132, 134, 143. *See also* humor
future tense. *See* tense

Gaffney, Gerry, 90
gerunds, 61, 64–65, 86, 111. *See also* headings; imperatives
goals. *See* message and purpose
graduate students. *See* students
grammar, 44, 102, 115, 133, 149, 151. *See also* punctuation; prepositions
Grammarly, 149
graphs. *See* figures
Gunning-Fog index, 37–38

Halvorson, Kristina, 127, 153
handheld devices, 18, 94, 108, 117
Handley, Ann, xiv, xv, 14, 22, 30–31, 36, 45, 47, 114–15, 137, 146
happy talk, 105
Hay, Steph, 43
headings, 58–65, *64, 87*, 111, 135–36. *See also* organizing
heat mapping, 150. *See also* eye tracking
help text, 94–95. *See also* forms
Hemingway App, 149
Henry, Shawn Lawton, 137
homepages, *105*–6, 110
Horton, Sarah, 30
HTML, 8, 59, 114, 120, 135–136
Huang, Kair-Ping, 22
humor, 126, 129, 133. *See also* fun
hyperbole, 55–56
hyperlinks. *See* links
hyphenation, 139. *See also* dashes

idioms, 126. *See also* colloquialisms
imperatives, 33, 61, 64–65, 85–86, 99, 108, 111, 117. *See also* gerunds
input fields, 91, 94, 99. *See also* forms
instructions, 2-3, 61, 79, 84–87, 91-92, 94. *See also* numbered lists
inverted pyramid, 26, 60, 104
irony, 126
italicizing text, 86, 139, 141. *See also* bolding text; emphasis

jargon, 35; avoiding, 45, 50, 55, 90, 107; removing, 29, 144, 147, 148; explaining, 43, 87, 152. *See also* terminology

Jarrett, Caroline, 90

JAWS. *See* screen readers

job postings, 70, 73, 130–131

justified text. *See* text alignment

key messages, 24, 77–78, 145. *See also* message and purpose

keywords, 102–103, 115. *See also* trigger words

Kimble, Joseph, 30, 34

Kindle, 7, 22

King, Stephen, 11, 32, 48, 149

Krug, Steve, 85, 105

Kupersmith, John, 15, 35

labels, 85, 92–93, 94, 99

layering, 27–28, 110–112

leading, 137

Lee, Kate Kiefer, 127, 130, 132

legalese, 42, 82–84, 92

Leibtag, Ahava, 130

letter spacing, 138

LibGuides, 3, 153

library speak. *See* jargon

links, 107–*9*, 120–21

lists, 63, 65–67, 69–73, 111, 137, 147. *See also* bulleted lists; numbered lists

literacy. *See* reading levels

Loranger, Hoa, 102

lowercase, 71, 152

Mayden, Shoshana, 153

measuring effectiveness, 149–151

meeting minutes, 5–6

Meirowitz, Claire, 114, 117

memos, 87–89

menus, 59, 64, 107, 111, 136, 140. *See also* labels; navigation

message and purpose, 21–28, 38, 145, 147; emails, 117–118; forms, 89–91; reader goals, 16–17, 21–22; signs, 79; titles, 56–57; websites, 101, 103–106, 110. *See also* organizational identity

microcopy, 94–95

Microsoft Powerpoint, 59. *See also* slide decks

Microsoft Word, 37, 59, 135

minimalist reading, 22. *See also* skimming

mobile. *See* handheld devices

modifiers, 32–33

Mom Test, 43

navigation, 60, 78–79, 84–86, 94, 97, 107–108, 136, 140. *See also* labels; menus

Neely, Pam, 114

negative language, 79–*80*

Nielsen Norman Group, 115

Nielsen, Jakob, 7, 22, 102, 107, 114–115

Nilsen, Kirsti, 12, 27, 137–138

nonnative speakers, 35, 46, 126

nouns, 49–51; active voice, 47; headings, 61, 65; link labels, 108-*9*; noun phrases, 50, 57, 78, 98, 118; strong nouns, 49–50, 130

numbered lists, 65–66, 72–73, 85, 127, 147. *See also* bulleted lists; instructions; lists

observations, 15, 152

openers, 114, 148

organizational identity, 129. *See also* voice; message and purpose

organizing, 25–28, 58–60, 145; emails, 119; forms, 96–97; instructions, 86; websites, 107, 111. *See also* headings; prioritizing

outlining, 145

oversimplifying, 18, 126

Pamental, Jason, 138

paragraphs, 29–31. *See also* sentences

parallelism, 63–67, 71, 85–88, 107, 111, 148. *See also* consistency; lists

parentheses, 31–32, 42, 45

passive voice, 7, 32, 47–50, 65, 78, 83, 87–88, 93, 106, 118, 147, 152. *See also* active voice

past tense. *See* tense

periods, 65, 141

Pernice, Kara, 108

personality. *See* voice

personas, 13–14, 22. *See also* audience; user research

plain language, 8, 15, 30, 36, 55

Polger, Mark, 79

policies, 5, 77, 79, 81–84, 106

posters, 1–3, 54, 62, 78, 109, 138, 139. *See also* flyers

prepositions, 34, 41, 49

present tense. *See* tense

prioritizing, 25–28, 31, 82–83. *See also* organizing

professionalism, 45–46, 48

About the Author

Rebecca Blakiston is a user-experience librarian at the University of Arizona Libraries. As of 2016, she leads a web team dedicated to improving the user experience through better content, design, and architecture. For six years prior to that, she provided oversight, management, and strategic planning for the library website as website product manager.

In 2013, she organized the certificate program in user experience for Library Juice Academy, including courses on usability testing, writing for the web, and content strategy. In 2014, she published her first book, *Usability Testing: A Practical Guide for Librarians*. Her advocacy and leadership is recognized nationally—she was accepted into the American Library Association Leadership Institute in 2014 and recognized as a *Library Journal* mover and shaker in 2016.

She has presented and published extensively on user research, content strategy, and writing with users in mind. She strives for clarity in writing and believes in the power of the written word to improve the human experience.